Leading with Light

VOLUME 2

A collection of thoughts from prominent light leaders

A CENTER OF INFLUENCE COMMUNITY
ANTHOLOGY

Edited by Lil Barcaski

Published by: GWN Publishing
www.GWNPublishing.com

Cover Design: Kristina Conatser

ISBN: 978-1-965971-06-2

Contents

Foreword

By Lil Barcaski

I love anthologies, especially ones of this nature, that allow people with similar mindsets and values work together to create one coherent manuscript. Even though each author in this book has a very unique take on life, spirituality, methodology, and modalities, they all share the desire to help others. They are all willing to share their experiences, their pain, and what they have learned in order to reach other people and improve their lives. Each chapter, while very different from the others, offers wisdom, insight, and valuable knowledge. Some of these authors have been very open about their life experiences, the pain they have endured, and their path toward the light. Each author offers something of value to the reader and it is my hope that you will take away a great deal by reading each chapter. Each chapter ends with a way to connect further with the author in a deeper way. Please take advantage of these offerings.

I am a writer by trade, an author, a playwright, and a publisher. The written word means a great deal to me. Words are more than just how I make my living, they are my way to reach people, to affect change, to affect the lives of others, to make people think and feel. I love books and always have. I love helping people become published authors and I have helped hundreds of people make that a reality. It is empowering for them and for me. Being an author has helped my clients get on stages, raise their business profile, and increase their revenue. It has helped them share their gifts and allowed them to help other in turn. It's incredible to realize how many people have been affected by the books we have worked on, like ripples in a pond. I love seeing the pride on the face of a new author when they hold their book in their hand for the first time and I love hearing their success stories once they begin to share their books with the world. Writing isn't for everyone but those that participate in the process of writing often find it's more enjoyable than they think and discover a love for writing they never expected to find.

Thank you for picking this book up and for reading the work of these brave and brilliant authors. Please share this book with others and become part of our Leading with Light family.

Lil Barcaski

CEO GWN Publishing/Center of Influence Community

Clare Williamson

Clare Williamson, also known as Solar, 'The Millionaire Sha'woman,' is a Conscious Creator, Bestselling Author, & Shaman.

Clare guides those who crave abundance, freedom, creativity, & flow with ease. She helps you shift from hustling and chasing success to attracting all you desire!

Working with the body, soul, and the divine to unlock your limitless potential as a Shaman, she blends ancient wisdom, sacred movement, and powerful soundscapes to awaken your Miracle Frequency —catalyzing a sacred journey of divine trust and magnetic attraction — a life where having it all comes with ease!

The Alchemy of Abundance

Unlocking Financial Freedom Through Sacred Sexuality

By Clare Williamson (also known as Solar)

In this chapter I am going to talk about something you may not have tried yet to reach the "holy grail" of financial freedom.

I thought about how to position my chapter in this beautiful book, *Leading With Light*... My own "lighthouse," for those seeking spiritual enlightenment, personal growth and to find solutions for their life and business...

I asked myself, what are most people seeking?

And I believe it is the "freedom" to know they can be "safe" financially.

It is why most people go to work every day...

It is why we push so hard in our own businesses...

And why we are always seeking the next thing and the next way to make more money or make more money more easily, whether it is through pivots in our businesses or job changes, or through saving money or keeping investments growing and safe.

But what I realised along my own journey was something so profound and hidden in this mental programming that has been so drilled into us from the moment we are born

It is easy to miss unless you consciously STEP outside 'the Matrix' and look back into it

And when you see it, it will immediately bend your reality and give you the financial freedom that you have been desperately seeking.

It is your own creative power. And I'm going to share the fastest way to access it.

Shall we first take a little look at the Matrix the way I saw it?

1. We are given a name to identify us.

2. We are given a number so that we can be tracked and served with all the systems and structures in society.

3. We are shot up on the day we are born with the first of hundreds of miracle drugs that have wiped countless diseases from the planet, so that we stay well and healthy.

4. We get supported by miracle innovations like milk formula and blended food so our mothers can break away from us and regain their freedom as quick as possible; so they can get back into the workforce.

5. Which is really what you are learning about when you get into school (earlier and earlier nowadays); all the things you need to know to be able to get a job.

6. Plus, the innovation of early childcare centres is a great support to get mothers back into the workforce earlier and earlier, right?

7. By the time you are into double digits you are already on a one-way track to employment. The only real question is... will you be good enough to work in the high corporate world? Or should you accept your inadequacy and head down one of the trade routes...? Because failing isn't an option. Leaving school

is illegal and highly shamed. So, it's really a choice of the first two routes so that you will be rewarded with a social security number that puts you in the tax system and opens the door to all the benefits you get from being a good citizen - getting a job, staying out of trouble and paying your taxes, so that the whole crazy wheel of society can keep turning.

Have you ever asked yourself when the true essence of you got lost in this whole crazy 'simulation' of security?

Have you reached the 'holy grail' of financial freedom by playing along with it?

Or are you like me and you started to see the cracks in the Matrix?

In 2015, I was pregnant with my second child.

I had a roof over my head, a two-and-a-half-year-old daughter already, a husband, and a mortgage we were struggling to pay on two salaries. And suddenly, out of the blue I lost my job. I'd been planning to sit back and enjoy some maternity leave, but all of a sudden there was none coming and nobody wanted to employ a heavily pregnant women. I got some part time work in a retail store, but it was clear really quickly that the salary was practically useless and the job would be impossible with a new baby. I was going to be without a salary with a brand-new baby. It was like a bubble burst. I felt unsupported, unsure of which direction to turn, but ultimately this was my first step into freedom as I started my own network marketing business working with essential oils, which led me into training to become a coach in 2016.

When I lost my job, my other daughter Eden was in childcare. She had been going there since she was one, so that I could work, which I had hated.

Eden and I hadn't had the best start...

When she was born, she was really unsettled. She would cry for hours at a time and screw her little fingers up as if she was screaming in pain. The doctors and the midwives told me it was colic, but at the appointment I'd scheduled for her six-week jabs, I was offered an alternative theory.

When I had been pregnant with Eden, I had suffered continuous urinary tract infections. I think I ended up taking five courses of antibiotics in nine months. Then she was born by caesarean. My new holistic doctor proffered that her little gut simply didn't have the right gut flora to digest my breast milk and so she was in pain. She suggested probiotics and not having the six-week vaccines.

"What?" I questioned her.

I was surprised, firstly because I didn't know there was a choice not to take them, and secondly because I had a lot of fear at the time around the diseases that the vaccines inoculated against.

The doctor didn't push my decision, but she asked me to go away, do some research then rebook if I really wanted to have them.

This was my first "awakening", and they only kept coming after that!

I invested hours into researching vaccines. Turns out they are not exactly what they say they are "on the tin", but I had to dig so deep into research papers to find that information.

It was scary. What else had I just accepted as "how things are" that was in fact not that way at all, and just an illusion painted by a belief system that I ultimately discovered I had deep inside…

That I was POWERLESS.

That made me follow a set of rules that were only there because I perceived my power to have security LAY OUTSIDE OF MYSELF.

Being made redundant at six months pregnant with my second daughter was my first step to where I stand today

Free from "the rules"

Free from the Matrix

In sovereignty

Aligned to my Soul

The road to getting here has required deep surrender that has often felt like losing control (and losing my mind) …

However, as I learned to let go, I began to see what had always been "planned" for me. I started to witness how everything that was happening to me, even when it felt scary and out of my control, was happening for me. I began to let go of how I thought things "should be" and began to embrace what was happening in the moment, without conditions.

And I began to see a divine plan unfold without me having any control over it whatsoever.

I ultimately realised that I was only yielding the control that my MIND wanted to have. I experienced ego death… ultimately, and allowed myself to fall into the loving arms of universe. The divine parent…. Source, Spirit or God; whatever you feel comfortable calling this.

As I describe in my own book, Awaken Your Miracle Frequency; It's Easier Than You Think To Have It All, where I share my full story, I spent my whole life fighting to have control because I feared the unknown.

As this awakening deepened, I began to embrace the mystery of life and of myself.

For the whole of 2024, under the direction of the consistent mantra, "Be Here Now," I rested in this surrender and saw my whole life change drastically. I walked away from my marriage that had ended abruptly the year before, I bought a Tiny House and moved to a rural farm, I let go of everything material and I began living in a way that felt aligned with my SOUL.

Another big shift was how I began to fully embody the 'lion's heart' that a true Shaman has. I committed to alchemical marriage with God through constant communion with nature and dynamic receptivity with my Soul's whispers, which came through my experiences every day. And I began trusting fully in the divine guidance that was creating such ease, flow, and abundance in my life.

In my business, I began to change my marketing messaging from "helping people to 'awaken a miracle frequency' that would support the same hungry chase to '7 figures'" that I used to have…

To… "working with the ancient wisdom in your body that creates this 'miracle frequency', deciphers your abundance codes, and aligns your life with your Soul's true purpose, so you can manifest the life that was always meant for you".

I TRUST from my own story that there is an unlimited source of creative power within our body and I am excited to show others how to truly tap into it to create a life of purpose, prosperity, and profound fulfilment.

All the way along this journey, Soul has guided me. And most recently it has felt like the guidance has been to simplify further. My business' offer has certainly become the simplest it has ever been!

"Simply", a community, resources and guidance you can receive if you are a conscious, creative rebel like me who wants to live your life in the most aligned way and change the world in your own unique way, with your god-given talents and nothing limiting your expression.

Especially your beliefs about money and how you create security.

That your belief *in* is a sacrifice *for* your most authentic creative expression and highest timeline of life.

If you are ready to swap the chase for success that traps you in a 'golden jail' - where you have security and some success, but lack deep soul happiness... For aligning with your true soul's purpose and breaking free of dependency, so you can unlock your innate power to manifest miracles...

If you are ready for a life of TRUE abundance

I have the keys to your freedom.

They are somatic.

They lie in aligning your way of being with the principle of **ALCHEMY**.

Alchemy requires a **CONTAINER**, something to **TRANSFORM** and a **FUEL** to drive the transformation.

The mere existence of alchemy means that change is always possible.

In somatic alchemy, your body is the container, your energy is what is being transformed and your own consciousness is the fuel to drive the transformation.

This means that change is not only always possible... But it is always available without having to lean on anything outside of yourself to create it.

This is where you begin to step into your true creative power.

The human body is so powerful. All of its cells, organs and systems create an orchestra playing perfectly in tune when everything is working perfectly in balance... But knock out one of the instruments - be it a cellular issue, organ issue or system issue - and the sound goes wonky. This manifests as dis-ease.

All of these things of modern life - birth intervention, giving up the breast too early, pharmaceutical medicine, processed food, even stress is knocking our beautiful orchestras out of tune. Even the buildings we live in are not conducive to balance.

I talked to a fascinating expert known as the Wellness Futurist about this on Episode 5 of my Podcast, *MAYU: Cosmic Currents for Conscious Creators*. Look me up and listen to it. The connection between architecture and the stabilization of your body's energy field is mind-blowing. A stable energy field is considered "harmonic resonance" or optimum wellbeing. Everything in the human body is just energy vibrating to create the form we know as the human meat suit that we all walk around in. The universe is created through the frequency this energy has, its vibration, and how it forms sacred geometry. However, we have become so human that we have lost consciousness of this energetic "being". We also abuse the part of our brain that was gifted to us so that we could make decisions... by over analysing everything and ultimately, distrusting in our body's innate ability to heal.

It also has innate ability to transmute the low frequency, dense energy that makes us need, makes us want, makes us fear, and makes us push, force and control... into a higher consciousness that restores balance in the body, creates a perfect flow of energy through the body that connects us to universe itself, and a Satori state that is magnetic to the constant supply of abundance that is available to everyone. This way of "achieving abundance" and the financial freedom you seek is a process that your brain, in the way that you are used to using it, is not required.

I call this Unconscious Alchemy. Which means the consciousness that drives the transformation that makes you magnetic to the life that was always meant for you is a Technology.

This divine power was known and revered by ancient Egyptians. They strongly believed in the significance of energy in relation to health, wealth and divinity. They even used sexual rites to transmute lower frequency energy to higher states of consciousness. The power of using sexual energy was in how this energy is self-created. As I have already stated in this chapter...

"Change... is always available without having to lean on anything outside of yourself to create it."

This is an area I have become fascinated about. Where your sexual power becomes your creative power.

I used to be ashamed of my sexual power until I realised that the energy of your sex is your energy of creation. It led to deep sexual healing, which I believe catalysed my significant change of reality in 2024.

This sexual healing enabled me to go deeper and more intimate with every element of life, so that every moment became sweet and worth savouring. I could feel this warm and loving feeling bubbling up as the smallest of things would light my heart up - how the light danced off the leaves, how the raindrops sounded on the roof of my house, or how delicious my dinner suddenly tasted now I gave it my full presence. I literally let go to love in every moment and allowed this deep love and a new level of trust to drive up my sexual energy into **EXPRESSION**. Unlimited by all the conditions I used to hold.

Can you connect with that feeling of your heart, soul and body lighting up because of something you love for a moment?

Maybe even close your eyes and bring a person you love, an experience you loved or something you are grateful for into mind and feel it deeply.

Feel your heart open... It is here that creativity begins. As you let go of your MIND and all its screwed-up beliefs and allow your creativity to have ultimate freedom. The lack of mind can feel like a void though because of how mind always externalises everything. It is constantly seeking to find a fuel source for what you feel on the inside. Your life is always filled with dramas and patterns you can attach to, so the mind can justify what you feel and rationalise it. And in rationalising it can map out your plan to staying safe. It can only do this from what it knows... from the learning it got from the experiences that you already had. And so, you stay stuck in an ever-revolving groundhog day of the same life, replaying the same patterns over and over.

When really, you feel abandoned.

You feel rejected. You feel ugly. You feel not good enough. You feel betrayed.

In these feelings you will find everything on the outside that justifies these feelings. People don't support you. You are unlucky. You are disadvantaged. Relationships won't stick around. You reflect your behaviour and choices to save yourself from the pain of these outcomes you already know will happen. When really, in doing this, you are only abandoning/rejecting/hating on/betraying yourself. I experienced so much grief realising just how many times I had done this. I realised I couldn't change the past, but awareness helped me to forgive the versions of myself that didn't know better, let those versions know she is and always has been perfect as she is and allow the pain of the experiences that taught her different to transmute.

Like me, you will have to heal and integrate your shadow aspects; all the parts of yourself that you feel ashamed about, the parts you find hard to love and the ways in which you fear judgement. But in doing so, just like the writers of the other stories you will read in this book, you will find they are your greatest **LIGHT** when you express them.

With renewed innocence, playfulness, purity, an open heart, curiosity, and love you will reclaim the power of your divine masculine and feminine energy that wasn't gifted to you so that you push and force your way through life, or become a victim to your experiences. You will come into union with yourself, creating balance and harmonic resonance, and remember your self-worth.

In doing this, you will activate **MAGNETISM** to abundance.

In the last year, in this way, I have experienced love flowing to me in the most beautiful ways. I have constantly been supported in ways I can't wrap my head around; I can manifest so fast! I've giggled at how universe can only say yes to what you ask for, so that when I have missed out key details in a request, I have received exactly what I've asked for, which hasn't been exactly what I wanted! I've also seen how you don't get if you don't ask and learned how to use my voice and not feel afraid to ask. And I have truly witnessed our divine parent in action... Like how a truly loving mother wouldn't give an excess of anything. Too much of anything is not good, right? So why do we expect to be flooded with abundance? We would we be given what we can't manage? We wouldn't. And the Divine Mother doesn't. She gifts us the experiences that teach us what we need to be taught. And when we rise out of victim consciousness and receive these gifts graciously with gratitude and love, our ability to manage more grows and we receive more, but we are also encouraged to stay in creative flow. Thanks to this observation, I've become a lot more playful with money. I am detached to money and don't place meanings on numbers. I know money has an inexhaustible source because it is energy, like everything. And I am the perfect conduit for energy to flow through. Money is just a form of energy flowing! We expend so much energy thinking about how we get money, which creates a wall to receiving it, and all the 'what ifs' and 'maybes' regarding how we hold onto it when we get it and spend it "responsibly", and it is just because we don't trust in the inexhaustible flow or our power to tap into it.

Your sacred sexuality is your deepest power to become part of this flow of abundance. Your unconditional love wakes up a serpent fire within that I am going to explain to you. I have been excited recently to be teaching people how they then harness and channel this power into their creative expression. This advanced manifestation technique connects you deeper to the truths of life, helps you let go of the mind, know love through being love, and allows your passion to channel that creation.

As I unleashed my own sacred sexuality, the meaning and purpose I'd always searched for... began to reveal itself to me.

This is how I know that everything you are naturally good at and all your effortless talents are not just random gifts, they are the result of something much deeper. You have been perfecting them for lifetimes. Your Soul has been travelling for lifetimes and has accumulated lifetimes of experiences so that you can also "Be Here Now", to live intimately into every now moment and channel your creativity to your fullest expression in the highest vibration of unconditional love.

But I'm guessing that if you are still reading this chapter... You don't.

You hold back.

You feel your Soul dancing when something you love comes into your now moment, but when you try to express through this love, something shuts down... you contract, you don't take action, and the creative opportunity is gone.

I don't know how many people I watched on Facebook, Instagram, Talent Shows etc expressing their art - music, words, movement, song - and I could feel my own instinctive desire to move in the same way, voice myself in the same way and express in the same way, but my throat felt shut down and my body felt locked up.

Physically I was also "shut down".

My neck, shoulders, torso, spine and hips were especially 'inflexible'.

I had a visible hump in my shoulders, no movement at all in my back and torso, constant pain in my shoulder blades and a hardening of my right ilium that was visible on an MRI.

When I experienced a trauma in 2021, I made the life changing decision to drop deeper into the breathwork modality I had been dipping my toes into with a community called Soma Breath.

In 2022, I signed up for their Master Coach/Breath Therapist course and began to learn more about bringing the body into the coaching I had been doing since 2016.

My "coach approach" had already slipped more and more away from 'traditional coaching', the more I was awakening spiritually, understanding the impact of trauma on our lives and also becoming fascinated with manifestation and the realm of the quantum.

I had delved so deep into this latter part that I had created my own 'QuNtum Leap Method' and certification in it to help people create change in their lives, but the amplified effects I was seeing as I brought breathwork into my coaching fascinated me. Especially in the area of creativity. I'm going to dig into this a little deeper for you so that you may understand how something like sexual energy can shift the things that are blocking abundance, harmony, and balance so fast. In a "quNtum" leap!

The breath bridges the mind and body.

When we use our Consciousness Technology to focus the breath, we create a chemical transformation that creates a dose of dopamine, oxytocin, serotonin and endorphins.

This is effectively what happens in sexual intercourse too - it causes the body to release its own cocktail of feel-good drugs that get you super present in the eternal now moment and in a higher state of consciousness. In this higher state of consciousness, you feel connected, blissful, and possible. A state of Satori.

Oxytocin is the love molecule. It is what's released when you feel in love and you feel passionate.

Oxytocin is shown to have the ultimate effect on the brain for neuroplasticity. Meaning you will change behavioural patterns faster when you feel love.

Soma's breathwork includes breathwork, positive mantras, music, other kinds of affirmations, and other techniques, so you can very quickly change your state, raise your vibe very quickly by changing the chemistry within your body, and programme yourself to wake up attracting the reality you want.

Not **NEEDING** and **LUSTING** for money (or anything) so that you can satisfy the body's primal need for certainty that you will survive. This is what society's systems and structures thrive on!

Instead, you begin to hold and enjoy each Now moment intimately. You transmute low frequency energy simply with your breath and focus. You burn through your fear of being imperfect and unsafe that blocks your expression for good. You move into a state of unconditional love and your lifeforce of creation channels your unique value to others, easily and authentically through your expression.

Which creates the exchange that brings financial freedom too. Your creative power. Available to you in every moment. With the need for nothing outside of yourself.

Ultimately, if you want to unleash your ultimate creative force and trust your INNER ability to bring form out of the formless... You have to embrace the void of certainty and guaranteed security. The intimidating "nothingness" this creates is the opportunity for everything to manifest. The uncertainty and the not knowing that come when you fully surrender all the patterns and beliefs that keep you safe and validated become infinite creative space.

This is the life I have now. True financial freedom because I know I can make money simply by following my heart in each moment, which is the gateway to my Soul, and for this there will always be an exchange in abundance in some way.

I am no longer chasing the Holy grail of financial freedom.

I am free Now.

Free to move as my heart, not my head dictates, comfortable in the void, constantly receiving because I am more creative and more magnetic than ever before. I have finally followed my passion for music and have launched myself as a DJ. I am learning the science behind harmonic vs. disharmonic resonance and its impact on manifestation, so that I can use sound as a powerful tool for creation and abundance.

What I am doing now takes everything I wrote about in my own book, Awaken Your Miracle Frequency; It's Easier Than You Think To Have It All to another level. This journey has required a deep level of faith, which is why in my next book, *Ritual Magick: Unlock your Ancient Wisdom, Sacred Sexuality and Untapped Creative Power*, I will show you how you achieve this important piece.

I am going to share every piece of wisdom I learned across two years practicing Ritual Magick to unlock the ancient wisdom in my body, my sacred sexuality and untapped creative power.

This is the forbidden knowledge that mainstream information won't tell you about accessing your true power. It's what they keep hidden from you on purpose.

And how I know that the true route to financial freedom appears when you close your eyes to everything you know and every way you have been taught and shown to make money and create security... and allow the earth itself to bring you home to the true power of yourself.

Before I said yes to this journey, I was chasing the freedom that would pay for the things I thought would enrich my life and I was constantly seeking the answers outside of myself. I was constantly in my head. Constantly thinking.

I craved to be a better mama… More present, loving, happy, and nurturing; creating experiences and memories we would all never forget. But in my business, we weren't creating any.

Now I trust the wisdom that is within me.

I trust that the energy that runs through me is the energy of the earth itself. I know my power. And I feel my path forward. Mother Gaia - my divine parent - provides my playground and the loving arms to keep me safe. The sun is my everlasting, ever giving protection and permission to live fully through my love and passions. I have taken my focus away from outcomes, completely. The earth holds me… All is present when I am present. I conserve but I do not preserve. And I listen.

Ritual Magick - song, dance, meditation, breathwork and music - has unlocked this deeper wisdom in me. Specific areas of wisdom that I am going to share in my new book; rites of passage, if you will, that got me to where I stand today. These rites of passage awakened the healing power of my heart, which opened the space for **MAGICK** while my mind took on a new role of being my balance and safe container to **CREATE**.

Life slowed down (or I slowed down life…)

I began using my masculine energy to focus my creative energy on aligning to an intention to simply express authentically, so that I stopped being constantly stuck in my head and trapped in doing, and I started living from my heart, acting on inspiration as it came to me.

Ritual Magick teaches you to stop, breathe, simplify and slow life down…

For Divine to come in, there must be space and openness.

In the break from holding and grasping, you can hear the breath of spirit guiding you and supporting you to move in honesty and truth.

You become an open field that spirit can touch and infuse with the magic that was always meant to bring your true essence to life.

I couldn't make up some of the things that have happened in my life to believe in this magic. I will be sharing all of my stories in my new book, *Ritual Magick: Unlock your ancient wisdom, sacred sexuality, and untapped creative power*, and guiding you through your own rituals and journeys.

Let's get one thing straight!

You are not the name given to identify you (that's why I changed mine from Clare to Solar!)

You are not the number that was given to you so that you could be tracked and served with all the systems and structures in society

You are not the damage that has been intentionally done by pharmaceutical medicine to your beautiful body since the day that you were born

You are not the abandonment you feel because the biological bond with your mother was broken too early, or because you suffered from the stress of her struggles and trauma

You are not the programming you received through school and a result of your own trauma and experiences

Etc. Etc. Etc.

You are not your mind.

You are a SOUL.

This story I will end with is not a story I have shared yet. Maybe I will go deeper in my next book… Maybe I won't.

I know all of this so profoundly because I met my soul incarnated in another body.

I felt instant love, the most intense love I have ever felt and it was the beginning of a journey I am not sure will make any sense to any person who hasn't walked it themselves.

I'm not even sure words will do it justice.

So, why, you may ask, am I sharing it?

The biggest reason is how it helped me love myself and I now know how important this piece is. And this is the place I know you need the most help, but will resist it. You don't see that your lack of abundance in any area of your life is connected directly to your lack of self-love and worth.

I never realised before I met Ben that I had so little respect for myself and so little love for the parts of myself that felt like darkness.

That is what happens when you meet your Twin Flame (one soul incarnates into two bodies who meet and catalyse a soul recognition that throws the feminine Twin into a dark night of the soul where she finally has to heal the things blocking her from her inner wisdom, self-acceptance, self-love, and being true to herself.)

You meet yourself, effectively. You see your shadows. BUT. When light stands with darkness, there is wholeness.

Meeting your Twin Flame is not about finding true love with your perfect person, which is so hard when you feel this deep love for the other person. It is about finding wholeness without your Twin and finally learning to love yourself without conditions. When you can do this, you will stop placing conditions on everything outside of yourself as well.

You will see yourself as whole and know you were never broken. Light and dark. Ben showed me that my unique qualities are beautiful, my voice has a place, my depth is unique and magical and my playfulness, adventure and wild spirit are my truth, however hard I have tried to run from them and push them down. Divine love is unconditional. That divine parent is you. Face your darkness, bring it into light with the deepest love for yourself that you have ever felt. This burning fire of love will transmute the lower frequencies keeping you locked in lower consciousness into the highest frequency of unconditional love, so that you come into integrity with your soul in your words, thoughts and actions. In this higher consciousness you will know your power, know you create your own security, know you are capable and worthy and will always choose love: to love yourself, choose yourself and allow the feeling of love, passion and joy in the most expanded ways. And know this love is never created by anything outside of you.

It's like the Twin Flame journey helps you finally see through the mind, and the tricks it plays and all the ways it has imbalanced the divine energy within you.

Essentially, there is no masculine and feminine when these energies within are in union. It's like the colour white is composed of all colours... Your masculine and feminine energy become one. In presence the heart opens and is charged and full. The mind has let go. There are no more judgements and expectations. Just experiencing and receiving. Being. And being truly seen. And as we allow ourselves simply to BE the form and conduit of life's force, then is why, and ultimately, when you and your divine counterpart can come into union in the physical also.

In one of the journeys, I will share in *Ritual Magick: Unlock your ancient wisdom, sacred sexuality and untapped creative power*, I realised that me and my Twin Flame were the Egyptian gods, Horus and Hathor, in an ancient life. Twin Flames will reincarnate thousands of times to finally learn the lessons of their shared soul. One of which Horus teaches is about wholeness.

Horus was so obsessed with being powerful and felt threatened by the power of his brother and so they were constantly fighting. In one battle, Horus loses his eye. Hathor helps him restore it, but she replaces both his eyes. She asks him to open his eyes and he sees love. He sees through light and darkness - the moon and the sun.

And this is such a powerful message to every Twin Flame. Both you and your divine counterpart cannot be in the darkness.

The role of the masculine Twin is to reveal the darkness of the feminine to her, so she can bring it into the light, and the feminine shows the masculine his light.

Ben has ultimately been the most powerful part of my journey so far in learning to love myself, to love unconditionally and start living through my heart all the time.

I never really understood what Ben meant when he said, "You can't lose me. I don't exist." Or why that hurt so much when he walked away.

Now I understand. When you know loss, you don't know your creative power.

Everything you are seeing in your world, you are creating. A fiction of your imagination, essentially. A picture that comes from your operating system - the beliefs created from your experiences.

When you feel love, when you love yourself first. Everything about yourself. You will see through the eyes of love; you will love everything you see and the magnetism that will create within you will pull in everything you desire.

Twin Flames represent the polarity of our divine masculine and feminine energies that blended, allow us to be in the highest frequency of unconditional love. We've all had experiences that have taught us not to trust and to close our hearts down to love. Feminine energy is open and trusting. It is how you allow and receive. Masculine energy is the strong arms around you that make you feel held and safe to express fully, including emotionally. It is the little 'push' of energy that takes your creative ideas to form. It is not the power and force that we connect to "strength".

It is still.

Napoleon talks to this in his famous book, *Think & Grow Rich*. He calls taking the emotions of our lower consciousness- i.e. a primal desire for sex, and blending it with the higher consciousness of love—sacred union of our divine inner powers—'Sex Transmutation' and he believes it is the hidden key to manifestation. The transformative power of emotions, that when blended, awaken the serpent fire that burns away all your limiting identities.

You might know this as "Kundalini Awakening or Rising." The sexual energy I have talked about that you have the power to move through you and in doing so, unlearn centuries of conditioning, so that you see the world through the eyes of your true self.

Which is love.

Each chakra is an emotional centre of the body. As your serpent fire burns through old stagnant energy - the suppressed feelings and unresolved emotions that prevent you from moving forward - you create room for light energy to flow. You develop emotional intelligence that will enable you to thrive in life. You release your fear of vulnerability. You open your heart fully to life. You develop a sense of inner peace like you have never experienced previously. And you realise it doesn't come with the material things being rich would have brought to you. You create a profound shift in consciousness.

Transcendence.

That amplifies your intuition, deepens your connection with yourself and universe, and creates a fundamental shift in your energetic makeup. You literally shift in frequency and life changes. I've experienced it. Everything looks different. You don't recognize the person you used to be and things that you used to happily co-exist alongside can't physically be a part of your reality any longer.

Honestly, this was really when I saw how I was just a pawn in a system of modern society that had trapped me by my fear. And it was the fear that I couldn't create.

And I was so hypnotized that I didn't even see it. I couldn't see that I was distracting myself from how miserable I felt; a misery I couldn't allow myself to feel because miserable was ultimately comfortable.

You might be there right now. Working a job that you don't really like or hustling in a business that you say you have so you can have more freedom. Or existing in a relationship where there is no connection anymore. Or numbing your pain with alcohol or other unhealthy coping mechanisms.

Ultimately, it is easier to sit on the surface of life like this, settling for the status quo, not truly aligned and not consciously choosing what would really light your Soul up. You have forgotten who you are. And the only place you will remember yourself is in the absence of all the ways you distract yourself.

The mind and Soul can't stay in battle forever. The Soul will always ultimately win. You will experience a tower moment like I did. Like losing your job or your relationship falling apart.

This is not because "life's a bitch" as the saying goes...It's because Soul/Source/God is always orchestrating your highest timeline. And for you to choose love. You have seen what you truly feel inside.

It will start with triggers.

People and circumstances that make you feel loud, noisy emotions. Soul is asking you to stop and feel so you can release what stops you from living the life that was written for your specific Soul Blueprint.

Sex transmutation "automates" this process. It takes the conscious mind away and uses the body as an alchemical container.

It bypasses what happens when you normally try to change things. When suddenly things are different and you suddenly feel fear. So, you fight back against the change. You try to hold on to how things were and you try to recreate the familiar. Instead of responding with unconditional trust in the source of divine nurturance, which is YOU.

You are Soul/Source/God.

And in trust of this divine being & higher consciousness, you can surrender & trust in the larger pattern that is playing out **FOR YOU**.

To get to this higher consciousness, you can learn the ancient secret of sex transmutation that Napoleon Hill talks about in his book, Think & Grow Rich. It is how to transcend your mind and trust in your body's intelligence at another level.

I would love to invite you to watch my intimate 3-part masterclass that unravels the mystery of why history's greatest achievers understood this force. And I teach you HOW to transmute your primal energy into pure creative power, so you can manifest your dreams and truest desires, and get fully on your Soul's path.

The real **SECRET** to manifest faster is not shifting your mindset. It is remembering that your body is a sacred technology. It is your access to and **TRUSTING** the little voice inside, which is the only voice you need to hear. It is transmuting the low frequency energy that is manifesting in the lack you have to the high frequency energy that will manifest the abundance you want.

It is the advanced practice of sitting with the reality and discomfort of your body's primal survival instinct and all of your programming and conditioning. Most of which is hidden until you step out of your unconscious pattern of life, create space for consciousness and master your innate power to overcome desire and unlock your creative power.

This is how I have personally shifted out of a life where I was sleeping awake in a golden jail; successful but unfulfilled and a pawn in the matrix trapped by my fear. A life that was filled with mindless distraction from who I truly am. To living my Soul's adventure of expressing my deepest **TRUTH** and creative authenticity.

If you are curious about harnessing the power of sexual energy for transforming your life, be it your business, how you create success, what/how easily you manifest, or even to improve your relationship, my intimate three-part masterclass is for you. It even shares the part that Napolean Hill neglects to share...

HOW to transmute your primal sexual energy into pure creative power.

I would love to invite you to watch my intimate three-part masterclass that unravels the mystery of why history's greatest achievers understood this force. And I teach you HOW to transmute your primal energy into pure creative power, so you can manifest your dreams and truest desires, and get fully on your Soul's path.

This is the link to the masterclass: **https://clare-williamson.com/lost-chapter**

I know that learning this ancient secret is the path to financial freedom that no one has shined a light on for you yet.

But what is even better?

It will completely change your life.

Kathy Bolte

Author, international Yoga teacher, Mantra Meditation teacher, Kīrtan musician, facilitator of wisdom circles, and leader of annual spiritual and healing retreats to India. Certified in Nada Yoga (the yoga of sound), Kathy has released three sacred music, and one mantra meditation albums, all available on most streaming platforms. In May of 2024, Kathy's book, "Ringo's Rainbow Journey: A Memoir of Our Border Collie's Return to His Soul Family" was published.

The Sacred Task of Finding Your Authentic Voice

By Kathy Bolte

What the heck is an "authentic voice" and how do I find mine? This is a question you might be asking yourself when you read the title of my chapter.

To be authentic is to be genuine or true to one's values and beliefs. There is an easiness about authenticity. To be authentic is to settle in to one's own affirmation about who we are and what we value. Our core drivers are the things that make us authentic. When we find our own authenticity, we feel assured, we feel liberated. We feel grounded in who we are. Our authenticity becomes our North Star.

Finding our authentic voice is a process of trial and error. It's an exercise of practiced learning that can sometimes take a lifetime.

Once upon a time, I learned that at the root of the word authentic is the word author. Authors are the storytellers. Authors are the ones who create the stories. Some authors write fiction, some non-fiction. Some tell a story that is scary or fearful, some write pieces that uplift and edify.

We sometimes use this word, author, to identify those who create, but not in written form. Someone might have authored a new way of thinking or a new approach to problem solving.

But here is the thing that struck me like a baseball bat upside my head: *I am the author of my life.* I can tell the story I choose, about who I am and how I move through this world. And through this process, I can find my authentic voice.

How empowering is that? I can author a life of struggle or a life of joy. I can author a life in which the main character (me) is a sad, mean-spirited person, lacking in empathy, or I can create my main character to be one who is kind, compassionate, joyful, and abundantly successful.

So, how does one go about authoring one's own life? Finding one's authenticity?

Seek your own truth.

Please allow me, dear reader, to talk a little about my own experience.

I was raised in a Christian home. Church every Sunday, youth group meetings, choir practice with my mom, bible study. My church family was wholesome, inclusive, and loving. No fire and brimstone. No mention of hell. If you loved God and loved your neighbour, you were good to go. Nothing beyond that to make me feel less than, or feel like a sinner.

In my 20s, I left Christianity. I'll get back to that in a minute.

Notice that I didn't mention my dad. That's because my dad was a less-than-stellar individual. He couldn't hold a job. He cheated on my mom. He was emotionally unavailable, and he was rather mean-spirited.

My mom did everything on her own. She worked, raised me, took care of our home, and was a beloved member of our church community. More often than not, my dad simply wasn't in the picture. When I was eleven, she finally made it legal and divorced him.

As I grew into my late teens and twenties, I began to do a lot of reading and exploring outside the box of the religious culture in which I was raised. My studies included reading the classic foundational writings of Plato, Aristotle, Nietzsche along with the more contemporary writings of Sartre and Simone de Beauvoir. I studied astrology, numerology, feng shui, transcendental meditation, and so much more. I became intrigued with the study of the Hindu pantheon and the non-dualist philosophy of Kashmir Shaivism.

Throw all that into a contemplative mix and you could say that I came out with a very eclectic spirituality, something quite different than the dualist views offered up within the context of Christianity.

I often say about myself that I came out of the womb seeking God. Wanting to understand The Divine has always been a driver in my life. And to this end, I began to get a grip on the importance of seeking my own truth instead of swallowing what my family and my American culture was feeding me.

LEARN TO NAVIGATE CULTURAL INFLUENCES

I am a 74-year-old American woman. My coming-of-age story happened during the sixties. I was smack dab in the middle of the counterculture, that rebellion against traditional values and norms.

I proudly embraced the hippie culture of peace, love, and communal living. The civil rights movement and anti-war protests became strong influences in my cultural upbringing. I watched in horror as JFK, RFK, and MLK were all assassinated before my eyes, shattering my illusion of safety.

Feminism became "a thing", focusing on gender equality, repro-
ductive rights, and workplace discrimination. I resonated deeply
with the feminist philosophy and I was all in.

I became obsessed with Bob Dylan, Joan Baez, The Beatles, and
The Rolling Stones. When the Beatles went to India, I also went, vi-
cariously through them. After the Beatles offered me an introduc-
tion to India, I became very curious about Eastern philosophies.
I read *Autobiography of a Yogi, Tao Te Ching*, and *The Way of Zen*.
My favourite novel of the day was Herman Hesse's, *Siddhartha*.

I tell you all this to say that I believe it is important to do plenty of
intellectual and spiritual exploration in order to become grounded
in discovering our own spiritual and social True North. Though
the cultural milieu we grew up in is surely a strong influence in
the development of what kind of person we become, we can make
our own discoveries and our own choices. Sometimes that means
walking a very different path than our parents or our community.
And that's okay.

As we discover what we resonate with, our clarity heightens, and
this gives us courage to walk our own life path. With enough experience, we become grounded in our values and beliefs. Our voice
becomes more sure, more authentic. We can truly begin to author
our own lives.

SPEAK IT INTO EXISTENCE

Do you remember when we were kids, sinking deep into the fan-
tasy worlds we created for ourselves? There was a magic word we
used to manifest our fantasies. We would say "abracadabra" and
use the waving of our little jazz hands to complete the magic.

Well, check this out. I recently learned that Ab'ra keDab'ra is a
phrase that comes from the Kabbalah which is an esoteric school
of thought in Jewish mysticism.

Here are the words and their meaning:

Ab'ra – I will create, keDab'ra – as I speak.

Let's say that again: *I will create as I speak.*

We create our desired reality through the words we put into the world, through our speech. In order to create the life we want, we can start speaking it into existence. Start envisioning it. Start believing in the fact that we are capable and have that power. That is our magic.

I'll give you a word of caution here. We'd better be mindful of what we think and what we speak because that will surely be what we create.

When we look along the spectrum of *new age philosophy*, we are likely familiar with the concept of the *law of attraction*. The idea here is that what we focus on becomes our reality. So, if we are routinely focusing on lack, on the negative or the disheartening, we attract those experiences into our lives. As we focus on abundance, compassion, love, we open ourselves to manifesting those experiences.

When we begin to get serious about creating good things in our lives, we must acknowledge that our speech, beginning with our thoughts, influence what manifests in our lives.

Let's explore an example of how negative thinking can sabotage our growth.

There once was a young woman (we'll call her Jane) who had been raised by a father who was emotionally unavailable and who criticized her constantly. Nothing she did produced praise, or even kindness from her father. Nothing was good enough for him. He often yelled at her, demeaning her and making her feel consistently "less than." She was never enough.

Growing up with this kind of negative treatment etched into her DNA the idea that she would never be good enough. She was programmed to live with low self-esteem. Her own self-talk further cemented this reality.

As she started dating, the boyfriends she chose helped reinforce her poor opinion of herself. She chose emotionally unavailable men. Though she yearned for a loving relationship with someone who would support her needs and honour her growth, she attracted men who simply reinforced her "not-enough-ness". She was never able to feel a sense of fullness in her relationships. Instead, there was always lack.

Her negative self-talk went something like this: "I'm not pretty enough. I'm awkward. I don't know why I think I deserve a good relationship. I have no talent. I'm not interesting. Everyone else is more fun than I am. Everyone else is smarter than I am. I'll never find a relationship that is good for me."

Because of her negative self-talk, she had invented many "shoulds" and "have tos". Her sense of herself was a subtle form of self-violence. Her self-talk was rarely kind. This caused her to act and react from her sympathetic nervous system.

The sympathetic nervous system is the part that locks us into the fight, flight or fawn mode. We react to our circumstances by either fighting against them, running away from them, or simply freezing and doing nothing.

The parasympathetic nervous system, on the other hand, is that which allows us to sink into comfort, peace, and even a blissful state. The parasympathetic nervous system supports our well-being.

Living in this state of negativity, Jane was far from a place where she could find her own authenticity. Not only did she have no idea what her authentic voice might be. She had no idea how to find it. Her habitual self-talk left her feeling sadness, disappointment, and even grief. How could she ever turn this around?

What Jane needed to come to grips with is that there was a deep yearning underneath the negative feelings. If she could pause and find the yearning underneath the sadness, she might find that her true desire was for happiness. There was a yearning to fit in, to be seen. She yearned for understanding and connection.

Jane began to sit with these feelings and she found that simply sitting with them, rather than running from them, allowed them to soften. Once these yearnings were acknowledged, they began to sharpen her focus. A great contrast emerged. She couldn't identify *what she wanted* until she was clear about *what she didn't want*. Once she got clarity about what she did want, she began to change her self-talk. Could she actually shift her focus from lack to fullness? From grief to hope and excitement? From being stagnant to moving into expansion?

Jane began to practice "reaching for a better thought."

Whenever her self-talk told her she wasn't pretty enough, she would reach for a better thought: "I am pretty. I love my long, silky hair. My body is strong and agile. When I look in the mirror, I easily see how pretty I am."

When she had a thought that she wasn't smart enough, she would reach for a better thought: "I love to learn. I read books that help me be more informed about the world. I once thought I wasn't smart, but now I know that I am very smart."

As she thought that she would never be able to attract a positive relationship, she turned that around: "I believe in divine timing and though I haven't found my perfect mate just yet, I know that the perfect man will find me, be attracted to me, and treat me in all the ways I yearn to be treated."

Jane practiced this often and soon she began to feel the fullness she had yearned for. She stood a little taller, laughed a little louder, was able to feel peaceful in her knowing that the confidence she was feeling now was serving her well.

With this newfound self-confidence, Jane decided to go to college and get her degree in teaching. She had always loved children and because of this love, she decided she wanted to teach young children. After getting her degree and her teaching credential, she was hired by a local elementary school as their kindergarten teacher. Her sense of confidence, coupled with her loving heart, propelled her to become an extraordinary teacher. In her third year of teaching, she earned the Teacher of the Year award.

Everyone could see how accomplished Jane was, and this didn't escape one of her fellow teachers. Bill taught second grade. His classroom was right across from Jane's kindergarten classroom. They saw each other every day and soon they developed a friendship which grew into a romantic relationship. They were married in a beautiful ceremony at the beach. Two years later, Jane gave birth to their first child. And, shall we just say, they lived happily ever after.

Jane serves as a great role model for us. As we reflect on Jane's story, it is clear that when she began to author her own life, she stepped into the lifepath that would serve her, and serve others. The genesis of the change in Jane came through recognizing that she was sabotaging her own hopes and dreams by continuing with the negative self-talk that was taught to her by her father. Once she began to "reach for a better thought", everything shifted for her. She began to develop confidence, began liking herself, and finally fell in love with herself and her life.

If Jane could do it, I believe that you, too, can do it. Here are some insights we might gain from Jane's journey:

Jane didn't rush things. She wasn't rushing to evolve. She realized that if she rushed, she was bypassing the negative emotions she needed to experience. She slowed down and savored the learning.

Jane observed what she was feeling. She tried not to judge or label. She worked on negating her own biases. She did her best to simply be a witness to what she was feeling. She didn't view her job as being the fixer of her problems. She was simply the observer.

She tried to remain curious. What was she feeling? What was she observing? What could her observations mean relative to her healing journey?

When the yearning and the pain became intense, it sharpened her focus. She didn't push these emotions away. She simply sat with them. Allowing herself to experience the extremes of her emotions provided a clarity that led to revelations about who she was and what she valued.

Sometimes our greatest pain can lead us to our biggest blessings, as it did for Jane.

CULTIVATING BALANCE TO DISCOVER OUR AUTHENTICITY

I've come to believe that cultivating balance leads to authenticity, and authenticity leads to liberation.

According to ancient yogic philosophy, there is limitless power and potential in the universe. This reservoir of power consists of three energetic forces that work in concert with one another to form the universe and everything in it. These forces are called the gunas, a Sanskrit word that means a *quality or attribute*.

It is important to cultivate balance in our lives, in order to discover the qualities that make up our own authentic voice. In order to understand this a little better, let's explore the nature of the three gunas and how they express themselves through human nature. These three gunas are rajas, tamas, and sattva.

Rajas is the energy of action, change, movement. When out of balance, this energy expresses as agitation or frenetic energy. A person who is overly rajasic tends to be hyperactive. This person may over-effort. They may be highly passionate. An overly rajasic person is often bound to attachments. Rajasic qualities could include restlessness, worry, anger or fear. A rajasic person often expresses chaos. On the positive side, rajasic energy could include qualities

43

such as courage and determination. If we think of rajas in terms of food, we could say that a very spicy meal is rajasic.

Things we can do to reduce rajas might include avoiding overly spicy foods, fried foods and stimulants such as caffeine. We might also avoid overworking and excessive consumerism, loud music and excessive thinking.

Let's circle back to our friend, Jane and look at rajas through the lens of her story.

As Jane obsessed about her belief that she was not good enough, she was overthinking everything. In order to avoid thinking about her perceived deficiencies, she spent her time focusing on her work. We could even say she became a bit of a workaholic. In order to keep herself alert and productive she always began her day with coffee, then drank a few cans of Diet Pepsi throughout her day. She craved spicy snacks so she munched on her favourite, Spicey Sweet Chili Doritos. By the end of her work day, she slipped quickly back into her obsessive thinking over all the reasons she would never find a good relationship. Her intrusive thoughts slipped into her sleep and caused her to be restless, at best, and sleepless on the worst nights.

We can see that Jane has become very rajasic. She realized her imbalance and decided to do something about it. But she overdid it and swung to the opposite side of the gunas pendulum and became more tamasic.

The nature of Tamas is dense and heavy. Tamas, when unbalanced, causes a state of ignorance and a dull, heavy nature which conceals our connection to our spiritual truths. Tamas is a state of inactivity, darkness, and delusion. A person who is overly tamasic is often lazy, helpless, and confused. States of depression, guilt, and shame may be present. Grief and dependency are also expressions of an unbalanced state of tamas. Lethargy and procrastination are the demons of the tamasic expression. On the positive side, however, a more balanced state of tamas can express as steadiness, groundedness, or restfulness. If we think of tamas in terms of food, it would be heavy, junky food with little nutritional qualities.

Some things we can do to bring tamas back to balance might include the avoidance of foods that are spoiled or chemically treated. Avoid overly processed foods, and no more heavy meats. We should avoid oversleeping, overeating, and inactivity. Try to stay clear of dangerous or fearful situations.

Let's look at Jane again. As she realized that she had caused her energy to become a frenetic version of rajas, she became sluggish and depressed. Her self-talk became very dark and even a bit delusional. She felt helpless and guilty for getting herself into such a dark place. She felt so lethargic that she began to put off the tasks she needed to get done. She procrastinated getting her work done, to the point that her boss found it necessary to council her. She craved carbs, carbs, and more carbs. Burgers, burritos, potatoes in every form, lots of bread with peanut butter, jam, and butter, these all became her new go-to foods.

Jane finally realized how she was sabotaging her growth. She devised a plan in which she would wake one hour earlier so that she could take a moderate three-mile walk around her neighborhood. She cut her caloric intake and began focusing on a more health-promoting diet. She ditched the fast food and incorporated more whole foods in her meals. She decided to give a vegan diet a try. In just a few weeks she began to feel strong and healthy again. And as for her mental state, whenever she felt herself going down the rabbit hole of negative thinking, she practiced reaching for a better thought. As she aligned with these healthful practices, she felt like she was becoming more balanced, more sattvic.

Sattva is a state of harmony, balance, joy, and intelligence. Sattva is the guna that those who practice yoga strive for as it reduces rajas and tamas. People who express sattvic qualities are joyful, peaceful, and compassionate. They have a sense of well-being and fulfilment. One might notice a cheerful, calm nature, and a sense of freedom.

To increase sattva, we do things to try to reduce both rajas and tamas. Eating healthy whole foods such as grains and legumes, fresh fruits and vegetables create a sattvic state. Practicing yoga and meditation are positive approaches to a more sattvic life. Enjoying activities that produce joy and a sense of peace are wonderful practices to increase sattva.

Jane's journey of bringing herself into balance led her to a local yoga studio where she created a regular yoga practice for herself. She found friends in the studio and included herself in their activities. A hike in the canyon. A night out at the movies. A meet-up for morning coffee and a leisurely chat. All these things added to her growing peace of mind. She was surprised to find herself feeling included. Little by little she began to feel valued by her community. She started to realize that she was a pretty great person after all. Her self-esteem grew and more often than not, she felt truly happy.

Awareness of the gunas can give us a roadmap to make more balanced choices and, just like Jane learned, it can help us find our way to our authentic voice.

THE AUTHENTICITY OF EMOTIONAL STRENGTH

There is an important idea that has circulated through the halls of psychotherapy for many years. That idea is named Emotional Intelligence. This refers to one's ability to have awareness of one's emotions, manage one's own emotions, and manage even the emotions of others.

Strong emotional intelligence gives us the ability to control our impulsive feelings and behaviors. Emotional intelligence helps us manage our emotions in healthy ways. It strengthens our ability to take initiative and to keep our commitments.

There are four components of emotional intelligence:

EMOTIONAL PERCEPTION – perceiving our emotions accurately. Is it shame or grief I am feeling? Frustration or anger? What emotion is my friend expressing with her body language?

THE ABILITY TO REASON USING EMOTIONS – I may be feeling listless and depressed today, but I have felt this way before and I know it is likely only temporary. Reasoning with our emotions can help us prioritize what we put our focus on.

UNDERSTANDING OUR EMOTIONS – this is our ability to discern what may be underneath our felt emotions, or that of someone else's emotions. It assists in the ability to avoid judging why we, or someone else, might be expressing angry emotions, as an example. Is my spouse angry at me for leaving the car out in the rain or has he/she just had a stressful day at work?

MANAGING OUR EMOTIONS – the ability to regulate our own emotions, and responding appropriately to other's emotions, are both important aspects of effective emotional management.

Let's see what Jane did with her emotions.

First of all, Jane developed **self-awareness**. She began to recognize her patterns of behavior. She learned how to name her emotions and what was motivating them. She saw how her emotional state not only affected her, but how it also had the potential to influence those around her. She began to recognize her triggers in order to avoid them and she saw that she had strengths as well as limitations.

Beyond the evolution of her self-awareness, Jane taught herself how to **regulate her emotions**. She learned how to pause, how to reach for a better thought, how to use the calming effect of her yoga and meditation practice. And, to her surprise, she found herself being able to mediate emotional situations that arose between co-workers and family members. When confronted with difficult situations, she rose to the occasion and faced them with confidence and strength.

Jane had lived within her dark place of self-doubt for so long, she was very motivated to make a change. This deeply held **motivation** caused her to seek many opportunities for personal development. She became driven to improve herself. She became propelled toward her version of success. Accomplishing her goals motivated her to set more goals to achieve.

As Jane began to step out of the darkness of her own self-judgment, she became more empathetic. As her **empathy** developed, she was able to relate better to others. When faced with rugged emotional expressions from others, she was able to see things from their point of view and this caused her to be a more compassionate person. She became less judgmental and more curious.

Jane's **social skills** became more adept. Her awareness of other people's needs and motivations came into focus. She became better at listening actively to others, giving healthy eye contact, and using her own emotions to enhance her communication skills. It became easier for her to connect with others, build good rapport and, most important, use a healthy dose of empathy.

PRACTICE GRATITUDE

The practice of being grateful has been highlighted in the cultural zeitgeist for quite some time now. Oprah championed gratitude. Brene Brown, Angeles Arrien, and even Emerson wrote about the importance of gratitude.

According to the culture of the "law of attraction" folks, gratitude is a wonderful way to attract abundance into our lives. If we are feeling lack. If we are feeling that we don't have enough of anything in our lives, whether it be love, money, freedom, or fun, we can learn to turn it around by truly appreciating what we have.

If we have a rocky relationship with a friend, we can focus on all the things we appreciate about that friend and feel grateful for those qualities we enjoy. Soon we'll notice that our friend is offering us more of the behaviors we enjoy, and less of those that have been annoying us. By focusing on what we're grateful for, we can attract more of it into our lives.

There is a simple gratitude practice I have been doing for several years now. Let me teach it to you now.

Take a jar. I like the acrylic ones you can buy at a craft store. They are about five or six inches high and have a metal snapping closure at the top. Decorate this jar to look festive. You can use paints, stickers, construction paper—anything that inspires you. Call this your **Blessing Jar**. Set the jar in a prominent place like the kitchen counter and place a pile of 3x3 note cards beside the jar. As you move through your day, notice all the little blessings that are presented to you. It might be something as small as a stranger in the grocery store doing a kindness for you, like getting something down from a high shelf that you couldn't reach. Or it might be something bigger like getting news that your employer has given you a substantial raise in salary. When you get home, take one of the cards and write this blessing on the card. Include some notes about the way it made you feel. Put these notes in your blessing jar.

Do this same practice every day from January 1st through December 31st. At the end of the year, pour all the notes out on a table, or onto the floor. Sit with these notes and read them all over again. I promise that it will delight you. All those little blessings that happened to you throughout the year are remembered. You can enjoy them a second time as you read and remember. This is a wonderful way to make gratitude a concrete practice in your life.

If you want to brighten someone else's day, why not write a personal note to them, letting them know all the things you appreciate about them. Send this note by snail mail. How many of us receive personal notes in the mail anymore?

As you develop your ability to be grateful, and to show appreciation, this quality of gratitude will become one of your guiding lights and will enhance the value of your authentic voice.

NURTURE LOVE

Of all the things I've learned in my seventy-four years on this planet, I believe the most important lesson is to actively love one another.

There is so much to enjoy beyond the love that a romantic relationship brings.

I've experienced so many kinds of love. I have love for my fellow humans, love for my family, love for my dogs and cats. I have love for the beautiful trees that stand so majestically in my yard. My husband and I planted those trees when we purchased our home thirty-seven years ago. My trees delight me.

I have a love for good books, for good food, for my sisters, my husband, my kids and grandkids. I love my home and the comfort it brings me.

I love my healthy body and my intelligent mind. I love my spiritual connection to all-that-is.

I love long, leisurely naps and a hot shower. I love a drive in my car while listening to NPR on the radio. I love good music and the variety of music that is available to us with the touch of a finger.

You may be looking at my little list and saying, "What's the difference between love and gratitude". They are similar, indeed. They are both emotions that elicit feelings of joy, but love is a little more complex, I would say. When we love something or someone, I believe we have a desire to care for the object of our love.

I nurture my trees, as an example, by making sure they have plenty of life-giving water, and keeping them appropriately trimmed. I nurture my dogs by teaching them how to navigate our human world to keep them happy and safe. I nurture my human relationships by spending quality time with my beloveds, telling them I love them, offering my help where I can, supporting their efforts at growth, celebrating their successes with them.

Gratitude, on the other hand, is the act of observation and appreciation. As I observe the world around me and all the wonderful things and sentient beings in it, I feel inspired, I feel grateful, I feel blessed. When I take time to be still in the present moment, I can easily find many things to be grateful for.

COMMITMENT TO DISCOVERY

We've explored several elements that make up the tapestry of our own authenticity.

Here is a quick summary of those things we've talked about:

- Be the author of your life.
- Speak your creations into being.
- Reach for a better thought.
- Cultivate physical and emotional balance to discover your authentic voice.
- Learn to navigate the cultural landscape to find your spiritual and social True North.
- Flex your muscles of emotional intelligence.
- Practice gratitude.
- Nurture the love in your life.

I want to add one more thing to this list, and that is the **quality of commitment.**

The art of discovering how to speak from a place of authenticity, learning how to move through life with a gait of assuredness: these things take a commitment to do the work. When we take steps to move through the muck and messiness of life, mine the depths of our emotional waters and find our own truths, we start to learn who we really are. As we get solid in who we are – who we authentically are, not who society believes we should be, this is when we finally become liberated.

And so, my friends, I invite you to make a commitment to yourself. Make a commitment to find your authenticity and take positive steps toward your own liberation. I promise, it's going to feel really, really good.

One final note, dear reader. If you enjoy my writing, I invite you to read my memoir entitled, *Ringo's Rainbow Journey: A Memoir of Our Border Collie's Return to His Soul Family*. You can find it here: **https://ringosrainbowjourney.com/**

Amanda Sowersby

Amanda is a radiant Art Alchemist who skilfully transforms darkness into light, seamlessly weaving wellness, truth, beauty, and goodness into every aspect of her work. As a multifaceted creator, she blends her talents as an Artist, Ecstatic Dance DJ, and yoga teacher with her roles as a meditation and sound frequency guide, energy worker, and reflexologist. Amanda facilitates workshops that inspire and uplift, all while running her own art and wellness school, Art & Alchemy, where she nurtures the creative spirits of both children and adults through art and artistic therapy. A true Crystal Shaman Dreamer, she embodies the essence of a moon child and sun worshipper, drawing inspiration from the beauty of nature to enhance her transformative practices. With each interaction, Amanda invites others to embark on their own journeys of self-discovery and healing.

Am I Truly Listening to My Heart?

By Amanda Sowersby

This was one of my darkest moments...

Seven years ago...

I remember driving home, the road ahead growing shorter as I neared the place I was meant to return to, but with every mile, my reluctance grew. A little voice in my head said, Don't go home!" Louder and louder, it echoed, "I don't want to go home." Yet I had to. My partner had work the next day. Responsibilities called; my boys needed me.

I stepped through the front door, and as soon as it closed behind me, something inside me began to unravel. My heart clenched, my chest tightened like in a vice, and the air seemed to disappear from my lungs. I could barely breathe. A panic attack gripped me, so sudden, so intense. I had never experienced anything like it before. Yes, I had my moments of overwhelm, but this, this was different.

I collapsed onto the floor, gasping for breath, my body trembling. And then, the response from my partner, it wasn't what I thought I needed at that moment. His words pierced through me. "Get over it," he said, "Pull yourself together." That was it. No warmth, no concern, just cold dismissal. My breath became even more shallow, panic tightening its hold. I lay there on the ground, utterly broken, as he walked away, leaving me alone in that terrifying space.

Just hours before, I was in a completely different world. I had spent two glorious, uninterrupted days alone by the sea, surrounded by trees and silence. I had found sanctuary in a secluded barn, far from the reach of phone signals and far from the city. For the first time in what felt like forever, I was just Amanda, not a mother, not a partner, just me. Free to breathe, free to be. My boys were five and six years old then, and I hadn't had a moment to myself since before they were born—since B.C. (Before Children).

That time alone revived me in ways I hadn't known I needed. The quiet allowed me to hear my own thoughts for the first time in years. I reflected on everything I had been pushing aside; the emotions and dreams buried beneath the weight of motherhood. Out there, with nothing but the wind and the waves, I found peace. I reconnected with a part of me that had been forgotten.

Things had to change. If you're reading this, you might be feeling that urgent pull yourself. Maybe you're grappling with a sense of misalignment, questioning your goals, or yearning for a deeper connection to your true self. You're not alone; many of us have experienced what I like to call "tense transitions" those pivotal moments when life feels chaotic, and we know we're ready for profound change.

On that day of the panic attack, my heart was in a state of contraction, my breath shallow, as if I were physically separated from my essence. I was at a crucial point where everything I thought I knew was unraveling, and I desperately wanted change. I felt the disconnect between my physical body and my astral body—the part of me that craved wholeness, healing, and a return to connection with source.

What do I mean by the astral body? It's the ethereal part of you that transcends the physical realm, holding your dreams, emotions, and intuitive insights. Ignoring its signals can lead to chaos in our lives. Think of it as a gentle wake-up call, urging us to reconnect with our true selves and find our balance again.

Have you experienced a moment that shook you to your core, a realization that your life couldn't continue as it was? This is where the journey of inner transformation begins. You may be facing the daunting task of confronting deep-seated trauma, navigating difficult transitions, or reevaluating your life. These moments compel us to seek support, to invest in ourselves because we recognize that something must change.

This chapter is designed for you, the seeker. If you identify with this struggle, then I want to introduce you to the transformative practice of art alchemy. During my own journey, I discovered that this isn't just a method; it's a pathway to reconnecting with and opening your heart space. Through art alchemy, I learned to channel my emotions into creativity, healing layers of trauma while navigating the tumultuous waters of change.

So, what is art alchemy? It's the process of transforming raw emotion, memories, and life experiences into creative expression, much like turning base metal into gold. Rooted in ancient practices and updated for our modern lives, art alchemy isn't only about making "art" in the traditional sense. It's about allowing yourself to experience emotions fully, then using artistic practices—whether that's painting, writing, dancing, or any creative outlet—as a way to transmute those feelings into something meaningful and liberating. This practice goes beyond words and thoughts, tapping into the depths of the subconscious where true transformation can occur.

Art alchemy isn't about perfection; it's about the process. It invites you to see yourself as both the artist and the canvas, allowing emotions and life experiences to shape you as you engage in creation. In the safety of this process, we can face our inner landscapes, bring light to old wounds, and emerge with a renewed sense of purpose and connection. Through art alchemy, we honour the full spectrum of our inner life, discovering that we have the power to transform pain, joy, longing, and fear into growth and healing.

So, why choose art alchemy over other healing methods? Unlike approaches that may offer only temporary relief, art alchemy fosters a deep, intrinsic connection to your inner self. It invites you to express your pain, joy, and everything in between through creativity, guiding you toward a place of wholeness and a renewed connection to source.

If you're asking yourself, "Do I have this problem?" if you feel the weight of disconnection, the ache of unhealed wounds, or the uncertainty of your next steps, this chapter is not just a narrative; it's an invitation. An invitation to embark on a journey of self-discovery and healing through the transformative power of art alchemy.

COMING BACK TO A PLACE OF WHOLENESS AND CONNECTION TO SOURCE

"The heart that breaks open can contain the whole universe."

– JOANNA MACY

This quote highlights the expansive potential of a heart that has undergone healing.

My pivotal journey of learning to listen to my heart and respond to it began with recognizing the deep disconnect I felt from myself. I realized that my heart, the core of my true desires, emotions, and inner guidance had been overshadowed by the demands and distractions of daily life. It took that intense moment of panic, that feeling of being trapped and unseen, for me to understand that my heart had been speaking all along, but I wasn't tuned in to hear it.

The heart is more than a physical organ; it is a profound centre of wisdom, intuition, and truth. To connect with it, I had to consciously quiet the external noise and the endless chatter of my mind. It wasn't easy at first. My thoughts were full of doubt, fear, and confusion, telling me to stay the course, to not rock the boat, to be what everyone expected me to be. But beneath that, my heart was whispering something different, something more aligned with my true essence.

I began the practice of regularly dropping into my heart space. This meant tuning into my body, slowing down my breath, and softening my focus inward. I used meditation, mindful breathing, and reflective art practices to create a direct line to my heart's wisdom. Art became a bridge, a way to express the emotions I could not yet articulate and to release the energy that had been stuck inside me for so long. Each time I engaged with art, I felt my heart open a little more, allowing me to hear its voice more clearly.

Through studying Anthroposophy and understanding the connection between the physical, etheric, astral, and spiritual bodies, I deepened my connection to my own inner being. I learned that the heart is a powerful guide, but only when we create space to listen to it, away from the chaos of the mind. I understood the importance of honouring my heart's signals, whether they showed up as discomfort, excitement, or a quiet longing for change.

Responding to my heart meant embracing vulnerability and trusting its wisdom even when it didn't make logical sense. It meant making choices that aligned with my deeper purpose, even if they were difficult or uncomfortable. This process brought about a transformation, leading me to reconnect with my soul's true purpose and passions in this life.

Art Alchemy isn't just about creating; it's about transformation. It's about embracing life's challenges and turning them into opportunities for growth and connection. If you're ready to break free from what holds you back, to heal, and to rediscover your true self, let's work together. Your heart knows the way, let's follow its wisdom.

Now, through Art Alchemy, I help others embark on their own journey of heart-centred transformation. By connecting to their heart through artistic expression, they, too, can discover what lies beneath the surface and begin responding to the authentic call within.

I've since learned to truly tune into my body and its reactions to different situations and energies. My body always lets me know if something is right or wrong for me.

I've learned to fully trust my body; it always knows what's right. When I drop into my heart space and let go of the mind's constant chatter, I feel an immediate sense of peace and grounding. Through my studies in Anthroposophy, nature, artistic therapy, crystal dreaming, yoga, and meditation, I've gained a deeper spiritual understanding of how the mind, body, and soul work together.

Now, I use artistic practices, healing processes, and the power of colour to bring myself into wholeness and help others connect to their own inner harmony. It's about listening to your heart and finding balance within.

DIRECTING MY LIFE: A JOURNEY OF HEART, HEALING, AND PURPOSE

That panic moment was transformative marking the beginning of my journey to my heart, a journey of profound self-discovery and the realization of my life's purpose. I was 35 years old then, standing at the threshold of a new seven-year cycle. Looking back, I'm deeply grateful for the learnings that came with that experience. It was through this journey of self-discovery that I was able to break free from the entrapment I had been living in.

Each step forward helped me reclaim my true self and find the path that aligned with At that time, my heart felt trapped in a constant state of contraction. On the outside, I appeared stoic, strong, resilient, like a good mama with two beautiful boys and a life that seemed "pretty good." That was true in part. But behind that facade, I felt isolated, alone, unseen by my partner, deeply saddened, and numb. I wanted to escape from myself. I felt trapped, as if I were merely going through the motions of existence, disconnected from my true self. My astral body, my body of light, was separating from my physical being, as if I no longer wanted to be present in my own life.

The concept of the astral body derives from ancient philosophy, where the astral body is seen as the part of us that lives on after death, and in sleep, it ventures into the spiritual realm to reconnect with higher energies. For me, that separation was happening in life. I was desperate for change, and I realized the only person who could create it was me. If my environment, surroundings, and even those close to me couldn't or wouldn't change, I had to transform from within. In my practice, I frequently observe sickness and disease manifesting within the astral body.

Drawing on my innate resilience and strong will, I decided to take control and redirect my life in a way that aligned with my true purpose. I knew that within every negative situation, there's a hidden positive, waiting to be transmuted. This inner transformation was the key to my freedom.

My mother had once given me a book as a teenager, where life was described as a movie, and we are its directors. As a creative, this idea resonated deeply with me. I thought, *What will the next chapter of my life be like? What kind of movie will I direct now?*

It was time for a new movie, a new role. I was ready for transformation.

We often forget that everything is energy, and our bodies react to the energy of our surroundings. In this case, my body was signalling that I was in an environment that no longer served me. I had been separating my astral body from my physical body, living in disconnection. But this moment was different, this was the moment I realized I needed to change, to take control of my life, and start a new chapter aligned with my true self.

RECLAIMING MY PURPOSE THROUGH ART ALCHEMY

When I first heard the words, "You're just a mum, that's just your role," said my boys dad. Something deep within me stirred. Of course, I love being a mother, but I knew I was more than that, I was still Amanda, with my own dreams, purpose, and a deep desire for self-discovery. That comment lit a fire inside me, pushing me to take action. I wasn't just going to settle into a role someone else defined for me. I had to follow my true calling.

Despite resistance from my partner, I pursued my training in Artistic Therapy, a dream I'd had since my twenties but was too young and inexperienced to follow through at the time. Now, with my children growing and a longing for independence, I knew it was time. The pull was strong, and I had to listen to it.

Through Artistic Therapy, I began to heal and transform. Art became my alchemy, a way to turn darkness into light, pain into purpose. It allowed me to reconnect with my heart, to listen deeply, and to rediscover myself. Art Alchemy helped me understand that sometimes life gives us nudges, whether through a passing comment or a moment of clarity, that push us toward what we truly need for our highest good.

One of those nudges came from an artwork I was shown: Raphael's *Michael and the Dragon*. In that image of Archangel Michael standing over the dragon, I received a clear vision of the action I needed to take; leave my boy's dad and reclaim my light. It was a moment of deep courage and clarity, and I knew I was being guided to make a change for the better.

That decision wasn't easy, especially with the guilt of how it might affect my children. But I knew that staying in a place where I was constantly dimming my light would make me sick and unfulfilled. Instead, by taking the hard road and doing the inner work, I found healing, for myself and for my boys. We regained healthy rhythms, and they flourished alongside me.

Art Alchemy isn't just about creating; it's about transformation. It's about embracing life's challenges and turning them into opportunities for growth and connection.

If you're ready to break free from what holds you back, to heal, and to rediscover your true self, let's work together. Your heart knows the way, let's follow its wisdom.

Now, through Art Alchemy, I help others embark on their own journey of heart-centred transformation. By connecting to their heart through artistic expression, they, too, can discover what lies beneath the surface and begin responding to the authentic call within.

> *"Healing requires from us the courage to face things, to take responsibility, to be honest, and to take the risk of saying yes to life."*
> – Nelly S. S. Sweeney

REDISCOVERING MY TRUE PATH AND PURPOSE

Why did I choose Art Alchemy over other healing methods? Because Art Alchemy doesn't just offer temporary relief, it transforms. It opens a deep, lasting connection to your inner self, allowing you to express and process your emotions through creativity. Whether it's pain, joy, or the nuances of life, Art Alchemy helps you journey towards wholeness and a reconnection to your true essence.

As humans, we live in cycles, each lasting about seven years. In Rudolf Steiner's Anthroposophy, this cycle-based human experience is one of continual growth and spiritual evolution. Each phase brings new challenges and lessons, pushing us toward deeper self-awareness. At 35, I entered my sixth seven-year cycle, a time of profound personal and spiritual awakening. It was the catalyst that led me to Art Alchemy, a tool that would help me reconnect with my heart and my higher self.

The heart, much like the sun, is the centre of our being. While the sun radiates light and warmth, our hearts carry the energy of love, compassion, and courage. But I realized that I had been living disconnected from my heart, trapped in darkness. I needed to change. By tuning into my body, I began to recognize how it responded to different energies and situations. Slowly, I realized that my heart had been guiding me all along, calling me to align my life with my true self. The path I had been on no longer fit, and this misalignment was showing up in my physical and emotional health. I knew that only I could make the change.

This was the start of my transformative journey, listening to my heart, following its wisdom, and rediscovering my purpose. It wasn't easy, but it was essential. Even though my external world may remain the same, I could shift my internal world, aligning my energy and actions with my higher self. Through Art Alchemy, I found the tools to turn my pain into purpose, to break free from circumstances, and create a life aligned with my heart's calling.

This is the journey I invite you to take with Art Alchemy, a journey of inner healing, self-discovery, and transformation through creative expression. Like me, you too can reconnect with your inner truth, find your heart's voice, and create the life you are meant to live. Art Alchemy offers the space, tools, and guidance to help you rediscover your inner light and step into your authentic self.

Rudolf Steiner's seven-year life cycle theory provides a profound roadmap to understanding our physical, emotional, and spiritual development. Each phase shapes us, offering unique opportunities for growth. As I entered the sixth cycle at 35, I experienced the most transformative time of my life, an awakening to my true essence. It was a time of reconnection to my heart, my higher self, and my purpose in this physical realm.

This journey laid the foundation for the work I do today, helping others reconnect with their truth. Through Art Alchemy, I support individuals in their own cycles of growth, guiding them to align with their heart's wisdom and rediscover their purpose. If you're ready to transform your life, embrace your true self, and reconnect with your heart, Art Alchemy is here to guide you. Together, we can unlock the profound wisdom of your heart and create a life filled with purpose and light.

> *"Art is a healing force. It can connect us to one another and*
> *to our own deepest selves."*
>
> – UNKNOWN

THE PURPOSE AND DEEPER MEANING OF SOUL MEDITATIONS AND ART ALCHEMY: TRANSFORMING DISCONNECT INTO CONNECTION

The lockdown at the end of March 2020 in New Zealand became a turning point for many of us, a time when we were compelled to retreat from the chaotic rhythm of daily life. As society was forced to stay home, I made the decision to take my boys to our barn on the East Coast of Wairarapa, a place where we could disconnect from the noise and reconnect with the essence of life itself. With no power, no running water, and no cell phone coverage, we stripped everything down to the basics. Our only comforts were a fire for warmth and LPG gas for heating water.

During those seven weeks of isolation, I dove deep into my soul work. I was studying and beginning my thesis on the moon and its connection to the feminine rhythm. Arriving on a new moon, I embraced the lunar journey of waxing and waning, allowing myself to meditate and observe the world around me, nature, plants, ocean, and animals. I immersed myself in the moon's light, attuning my awareness to its rhythms, both externally and internally. Each day, I created multiple artworks as part of my soul meditations, a practice that helped heal my irregular sleep patterns and allowed my menstrual cycle to synchronize with the moon's phases. I discovered that the moon was working on my lower metabolic and unconscious realms, guiding me toward deeper self-awareness.

Every morning, I would rise just before sunrise, walking through the pine trees to my favourite spot, a tranquil place overlooking the ocean. Here, I would meditate, chant, breathe, and simply be. This intentional practice, coupled with going to bed at twilight, aligned me with the natural rhythm of the sun. Each sunrise brought its own unique energy and colour, and on Easter Sunday, as I stood at the top of a hill, I waited for the moment of dawn. When the sun broke over the horizon, it was profound; I felt my heart expand, and an awakening occurred within me, connecting me to the Divine. In that moment, I realized that even while studying the moon, it was the sun's powerful forces that were deeply influencing my consciousness.

The moon, in its subtlety, reflects the sun's energies and the energies of other celestial bodies back to us on Earth. This duality, the interplay of sun and moon, symbolizes the balance of yin and yang, masculine and feminine, warmth and coolness. Together, they hold hands in a cosmic dance, reminding us of the essential balance we need in our own lives.

During this transformative period, I created some of my most meaningful soul artworks, which I now share with others through healing art. I discovered that when our natural rhythms with the cosmos and our surroundings are disrupted, illness sets in. This imbalance is further exacerbated by the busyness of modern life and the myriad distractions technology presents. As Margarethe Hauschka aptly noted, "Our time is tearing the soul to pieces and creating uncertainty and desolation in the soul." The artistic process becomes a vital antidote, helping to relieve and rebalance the disturbances that disrupt our inner peace.

In connecting to our heart through soul meditations is a transformative journey. By engaging with nature and creativity, we turn disconnection into connection, exploring our depths and transforming darkness into light. This process not only heals us but also inspires others on their paths.

WHAT IS ART ALCHEMY?

As Rumi beautifully states, *"The wound is the place where the Light enters you,"* reminding us that our pain can lead us to profound insights and healing.

Art Alchemy is more than just a practice, it's a way of being that I've crafted from years of learning, teaching, and deep personal exploration. It's a transformative blend of healing methods and spiritual wisdom, designed to guide you back to your inner self. Through the power of colour, energy work, breathwork, grounding techniques, and chakra balancing, I help you tap into the profound connection between the body, mind, and spirit.

This is more than just a practice; it is a sacred journey of self-discovery that empowers individuals to reconnect with their deepest selves and transform their experiences into profound wisdom. A journey from dark to light through the process of creative expression, we access the hidden layers of our hearts, allowing us to navigate the complex landscape of our emotions, desires, and truths.

Inspired by the natural world, Art Alchemy weaves in the healing energies of the plant, mineral, and animal kingdoms. I also integrate yoga, sound healing, and crystal dreaming, alongside shamanic practices, all aimed at aligning you with the higher qualities of truth, beauty, and goodness.

This journey is about more than just healing; it's about reconnecting with the deepest parts of yourself and the universe. With Art Alchemy, you're not just finding balance, you're awakening to your true essence, your purpose, and the beauty that resides within. Let's embark on this profound journey together.

This journey encourages us to listen closely:

Is it my heart talking?

Am I truly connected to my heart's wisdom?

"Creativity takes courage."

– HENRI MATISSE

I love this quote as it reminds us that engaging in creative processes is a brave step towards healing.

As we engage with this transformative art, we begin to unveil the whispers of our hearts, guiding us toward clarity, purpose, and healing. In a world filled with distractions and chaos, this connection becomes our anchor, a powerful reminder that our hearts are the bridge between our earthly experiences and our spiritual essence

OPENING MY HEART AND LISTENING TO ITS WISDOM: EXAMPLE OF MY WORK:

In my work, I frequently encounter clients who ask, "How do I know if it's my heart talking? How can I connect to my heart?" This inquiry often marks the beginning of their transformative journey. Understanding the distinct voices of the mind, heart, and gut, or lower metabolic area, is crucial in navigating this path.

UNDERSTANDING THE VOICES WITHIN

To start this journey, it's essential to identify the source of our thoughts. I help clients discern whether their thoughts are their own or influenced by external factors. Introducing thought consciousness allows them to recognize that many thoughts are projections from the outside world.

Guided meditations are effective for this understanding. Calming the nervous system and practicing conscious breathing create a space for self-reflection. In high-stress states, we often disconnect from our bodies and hearts, making it hard to hear our true guide.

BALANCING THE ENERGIES

The heart serves as a bridge between the earthly and spiritual realms, facilitating deeper emotions and intuition. As the fourth chakra, or Anahata, it connects us through the colours green and pink. I work with a broader spectrum of twelve chakras, where lower chakras ground us physically, and upper chakras link us to spiritual realms.

In my practice, I assess the balance of my clients' chakras using crystals and sound healing tools to unblock stagnant energy. Colour plays a vital role in emotional and physical healing.

For example, I worked with an 11-year-old girl coping with grief from her parents' separation through playful pastel exploration. This creative process eased her heart's heaviness, allowing her to express her feelings and create art that reflected her healing journey.

We possess both a spiritual and a physical heart. The physical heart beats within us, while the energetic heart radiates energy several feet beyond our body. Highly sensitive individuals can often sense this energy.

I also use Crystal Dreaming, a shamanic meditation that removes blockages to heart connection. Healing trauma is crucial for accessing our deeper selves and transforming negative experiences into positive insights.

THE PROCESS OF CRYSTAL DREAMING

During a Crystal Dreaming session, clients lie or sit within a crystal mandala for energetic protection and activation. This process reveals where trauma or blockages reside, facilitating release and connection to our higher selves.

In one session, a client struggled to connect to her heart due to a blockage in her throat. By focusing on healing this area during meditation, she was able to release stored trauma, ultimately connecting with her heart, a significant breakthrough!

This illustrates how blockages in one area can disrupt the entire body. By releasing these blockages, we create pathways for energy to flow freely, helping us reconnect with our heart's wisdom.

When I began working with clients, I was still healing from past wounds and unsure how to protect my heart. Despite using natural remedies, I realized true transformation needed to come from within. We possess both a spiritual and a physical heart. The physical heart beats within us, while the energetic heart radiates energy several feet beyond our body. Highly sensitive individuals can often sense this energy.

As an intuitive Art Alchemist, I sense the emotions of others. Initially, I struggled to shield myself and often carried their pain. Over time, I developed a spiritual practice that allows me to connect deeply with clients without losing my sense of self. This is called spiritual hygiene and is a very important daily tool when working as a therapist.

THE ALCHEMY OF THE HEART

Through art practices that resonate with the heart, body, and spirit, I facilitate self-exploration and nurture the connection between the physical and spiritual selves. Clients learn to listen to their hearts and trust their inner wisdom, paving the way for significant transformation.

In this creative space, we discover that our hearts hold the key to our true purpose. By embracing the transformative power of Art Alchemy, we heal wounds and find joy and authenticity.

Healing and listening to the heart can happen at any point in life. The call to connect with your heart's wisdom serves as an invitation to explore your true self and desires.

The journey of the heart continuously evolves. If you seek deeper connection and healing, Art Alchemy offers a powerful means to access that wisdom. This sacred practice transforms pain into light and confusion into clarity, unlocking your potential.

This journey prompts us to listen: Is it my heart speaking? As we engage in transformative art, we unveil the whispers of our hearts, guiding us toward clarity and healing.

I warmly invite you to awaken your inner wisdom as you embrace the next chapter of your life, guided by the gentle truths of your heart. Together, let's embark on this beautiful journey where your heart's voice will resonate, allowing your authentic self to shine brightly. Reach out to me today, and let's begin this transformative exploration into the alchemy of your heart. Your heart is ready, let's uncover its profound wisdom and unlock its full potential together.

Connect with me:

www.amandaartworks.com

www.artandalchemy.co.nz - to be live soon

Facebook: Amanda Sowersby

Amanda Sowersby Art & Artistic Therapy

Instagram: @amandasowersby

Email: amanda@artandalchemy.co.nz

amandasowersby@gmail.com

Jess Reidell

Jess Reidell was a co-author in Leading with Light Volume one and helped create the "Leading with Light" concept to support more light workers and thought leaders with creating a legacy through sharing their unique message with the world. She is a certified Life Coach who received her training from the Martha Beck Institute. Jess graduated from Roanoke College with a BA in Theatre and received her MFA in Acting from Louisiana State University. She specializes in supporting clients with navigating major life transitions such as divorce and career change. With her strong intuition and clairaudience, she guides her clients with unique tools to create self-trust and sovereignty to live intuitively inspired and "ageless" lives.

Jess lives in Dunedin Florida with her husband Dave and their mischievous American Eskimo Dog, Cinco.

No Coincidences Only Synchronicities

By Jess Reidell

"THERE ARE NO COINCIDENCES ONLY SYNCHRONICITIES"

I'm kicking off this chapter with a confession. There was a time in my life when I didn't really believe in magic and miracles. In my 20's and 30's I essentially felt like a victim of circumstances. I walked through life this way, feeling frustrated and annoyed that my life was not as I would have liked it to be. This was before I understood that we are actually the conscious creators of our own lives. In my 40's, I came to understand that the key to seeing magic and miracles starts with the belief that miracles are possible. Once I chose to be fully open to the possibility of real magic and miracles being a part of MY OWN LIFE the evidence began to appear, then it practically started to pile up. I realized the truth of the phrase "There are no coincidences, only synchronicities." I read that sentence in Radleigh Valentine's *How to be Your Own Genie* in 2017 and I've never forgotten it. Here are a few of the remarkable examples from my own life that served to reinforce this belief for me. Prepare for some magic and awe of your own.

THE CASINO STORY

It was a steamy summer night in June of 2022. June 13th, to be exact. The month prior my husband, dog and I had just settled into our new home in Florida. We had some friends in town who were staying at a local hotel and we decided to take them to the casino for dinner and fun.

My husband and I have always enjoyed the casino. I'm actually the one who got him into it. Our favorite place to vacation when we lived in Atlanta was Biloxi, Mississippi. When we would play roulette he would always play red 18, for his deceased brother James, who was born on June 18th and whose life was taken by a tragic accident on June 3rd, 1996.

"18 for brother James!" he would say, blowing on the chip before laying it on the table.

After eating, we all went for a little casino play. I put a twenty-dollar bill into a game I like called "Outback Bucks." When you get to the bonus round, you hear the sound of a horn and a Kangaroo comes jumping down into the frame. Sometimes, you get a second bonus where you get to spin and get as many symbols as you can and if you get them all, the jackpot doubles. A few spins in the machine goes crazy. The "Grand" jackpot fell into the last frame and then everything doubled. I was sitting there in awe. I had won a whopping $4400.

I had them pay me out in $100 bills. I've always wanted to do that, have a casino employee "make it rain" with my winnings. My friend took a video. In the video I'm breathing so deeply you can see my chest rise and fall, I was beyond excited. I tipped him $40. There was a woman at a machine that was catty corner to me who was cheering on my win in awe. She had a "to go" box in her lap. We had chatted while I was awaiting my cash payout. After I got the cash I took my friends to the bar and bought them a round of drinks. I handed my girlfriend $40 as she was distressed that she had lost it playing slots. I then played a couple more machines, lost about $80 and then I turned to my husband and said "Let's go, I don't want to lose any more of this jackpot!" I know from experience that it is dangerous and tempting to keep gambling when you are on the "high" of a big win so we all beat a path out of the casino before I could do any more damage.

At the time, I was wrestling with leaving a job that I was miserable at. I get that misery is a choice, but when I examined my life, every part of it made sense and was extremely fulfilling, with the exception of this particular employment opportunity. I was experiencing a good bit of fear about not having "enough" money if I were to leave and start my own business again. Something about winning that jackpot felt like a sign from the heavens that everything was going to be okay.

The following Thursday, I decided to go back to the casino and try my luck. I drove out there, enjoyed a solo dinner and started playing a bit. I wasn't winning much or losing much either, but having fun nonetheless. I had almost thrown in the towel and was deciding to wend my way back to the parking garage when I walked past my "Lucky Machine" from the previous Saturday. The same one. The Outback Bucks machine.

Lightning doesn't typically strike in the same place twice now, does it? I asked myself as I sat down. Just a couple of minutes in, the Kangaroo jumped on down and I was in another bonus round. Following a noisy commotion on the part of the machine, I hit another jackpot. This time it was $6600.

I took a snapshot of the machine and sent it to Dave with the caption "Oops, I did it again!" He immediately called me. I told him, "I'm not believing this." This time I was smarter and asked for $500 cash and the rest in the form of a check. And let me tell you, that check took a while. As I was waiting, I looked over to the person seated at the machine that was catty corner to mine. Unfuckingbelievable. It was the SAME WOMAN who had been sitting in the EXACT SAME PLACE when I won on Saturday night.

"It's YOU!" I exclaimed.

"It's YOU!" She said back to me incredulously. She actually had a "to go" box on her lap just like she did on Saturday night and for a minute I wondered if I was in the twilight zone.

The casino employee finally returned with my check and cash. This time, I gave the lady some money and thanked her for being a lucky charm. I left shortly thereafter. When I look at the W2 form I noticed the date. It was June 18th, Brother Jame's birthday.

Dave and I had been toying with the idea of buying a golf cart and once I won the second jackpot we moved forward with getting one. When we were working on our taxes he noticed the date on the W2 form also. He said he hadn't realized it had happened on Brother Jame's birthday. This had not gone unnoticed by me.

"There are no Coincidences, only Synchronicities."

RAINBOWS

After a sunny beautiful September day on Honeymoon Island beach in Dunedin, we brought some visiting friends downtown to catch the Sunset and go to dinner. It had rained in the late afternoon, and on this particular evening there was a gorgeous double rainbow over the town.

I stared at that beautiful double rainbow and made a wish. It's the wish I've made since I was 22 years old while in graduate school in Louisiana, when I threw a coin into a fountain at Mardi Gras. I wish it every time I blow out a candle or see a shooting star. As I write this it's occurring to me, I sound rather superstitious. I guess to some degree all mystics are.

The wish, which became my life motto, is simple.

"I hope I always have a great time, NO MATTER WHAT."

This gives me great comfort when things appear to go sideways in my life. It's helped me make the best out of many unfortunate and disappointing situations. I also now live by the creed that we cannot let our circumstances define us, nor can we bend in the breezes and react every time things don't go our way.

So, I stared up at that gorgeous double rainbow and made a wish.

"I hope I always have a great time no matter what."

For good measure, I threw in another.

"I hope everything works out the way it's supposed to."

That one was relevant because, two days later, I was to travel to another state to give notice to the job that no longer aligned with my sunny, rainbow-filled world. I had decided to go back into business for myself, and I had seen first-hand how challenging that could be. I had some trepidation around it, fears about not having enough sustainable work on my own. Normal stuff.

What happened next was one of the most incredible experiences I had ever had in the 51 years I had been on the planet at that point.

As we were walking to dinner, I began noticing that every light I saw had a RAINBOW around it. These were not subtle rainbows, mind you, rather, vibrant, bright beautiful rainbows. Surrounding every light I laid eyes on.

Headlights, streetlights, candlelight. Even a chandelier in the restaurant had each light surrounded by a brilliant rainbow. The whole experience was surreal. I started to describe what I was seeing to Dave and my friends. They looked at me kinda funny.

"Are you sure you don't have a brain tumor?" my husband asked.

"I don't see any rainbows." my girlfriend said.

"I don't see any either." Her husband stated.

"This is INCREDIBLE," I said with awe.

I guess it is pertinent to share that I wasn't on drugs, because you're probably wondering that at this point. This wasn't some psychedelic trip with chemicals or hallucinogens. A bit of alcohol, yes, but not an amount that would have me seeing rainbows everywhere.

I kept trying to rationalize it myself. "Maybe it's something going on with my contacts." I speculated. But when the contacts came out that night, I opened my front door and the rainbows were still there, circling the neighbors' lights across the street and even around… wait for it. The MOON.

My friend Danielle, a fellow intuitive, shared with me that she typically sees faint rainbows around most lights. I was hopeful that I would too. The following day, the rainbows were much fainter, even though I could still make them out in the daylight. On Monday night after flying to North Carolina, I stared up at a streetlight after dark and could see one rainbow that was very faint.

The next day, nothing.

It was magical, yet bewildering.

Months later, I spoke to my eye Doctor about it. She could not come up with a medical reason for that to happen and everything with my vision exam checked out. I can only conclude that this was a miracle of sorts. Having taken this glimpse into this visually magical alternate universe, I can't wait for the day to come that the rainbows appear again. And this time, maybe they'll stay.

There are No coincidences, Only synchronicities.

THE HUSKY STORY

It was March of 2024. The afternoon started off with a big ugly cry. I had just finished up a coaching call, one where I was being coached, not the other way around. The person doing the coaching was my practice partner from my Martha Beck Coaching program who is now a dear friend, so she knows me pretty well. I had a couple pretty big bedrock epiphanies about my resistance to taking action and the whole thing ended up with some major breakthroughs on my part. And the big ugly cry. And it looked like the Universe had something different in store for me that day to show me what "action" really looks like. Read on.

After the coaching session, I went outside to walk my dog, Cinco. I ran into a guy in my neighborhood who has a male Husky. Cinco happens to hate the Husky, and she normally barks and growls and acts up when she sees him. I usually feel slightly embarrassed about my dog's behavior and this sweet man, without fail, always tells me to "have a blessed day."

So I saw the man and addressed him from across the street.

"How are ya?" I said.

"Stressed," he answered.

"Wait…" I said, because at first I thought he said "Blessed," because that's what he normally says. But that day he threw me off.

"What?" I asked. "Stressed and not blessed?"

"I have to take my dog to the pound this afternoon. I've been crying about it for days." He told me.

"Wait—WHUT? Whut are you talking about? You love that dog!" I exclaimed.

"I do, but he broke through his crate and I can't afford another one right now. The one he needs is several hundred dollars. I need to be out of the house tomorrow all day for my medical appointments. I can't leave him alone if he's not in the crate, he'll destroy my whole house."

"Have you tried posting about it? See if someone has something they could donate to get you through?" I asked.

"I'm not online," he answered. "I've called around to all the veterinarians in the area and can't get any help."

"Let's pray for a miracle" I said.

"Well, It'll have to happen in the next couple of hours." He said. "I'll need to take him and drop him off this afternoon."

The gravity of this whole situation hit me. I imagined having to give up Cinco and I got this sharp pang in my heart.

"What's your house number?" I asked him. He told me.

"Tell you what. Don't do anything yet. Give me til the end of the day. I'll see what I can do." I replied.

I went into the house and jumped on Facebook and Next Door, quickly typing a synopsis of what was happening and asking if anyone had a large crate they could spare. Then I walked over to find his house (or what I thought was his house) but apparently I had inverted the numbers and was looking for a house that doesn't exist on my street.

My heart sank. I couldn't believe my sieve-like brain. *If I can't find the house, that's going to be a problem.*

I considered knocking on some doors, asking if people knew which house the guy with the Husky lives in, but then it occurred to me he might not be back from his walk yet. I see two Dudes cruising by on bicycles and I yelled, "Hey! Did you see a guy with a Husky?"

"Yes!" One of them yelled back. "He's at the park!"

Whew. Close call. I started booking it towards the park and I saw him coming my way. We walked back together.

We went into his house and he showed me the damage. I took a few photos of the crate.

It turned out he was a disabled veteran. He had diabetes. He said that walking the dog for a mile a day is his exercise. He lived alone and has had the dog, whose name is "Bandit" for four years. He showed me some of Bandit's medications.

"Is there any part of you that really wants to give up this dog?" I asked him. "Do you have everything you need right now except the crate?"

"No. I want to keep him. I have plenty of food for him. I just can't leave him alone tomorrow. He has separation anxiety. He'll tear up the house."

I got his number and added him as a contact in my phone. I had an appointment to do some leg compression so I grabbed my laptop and headed to the facility, my head spinning and my wheels turning. I thought of a friend who works with disabled veterans so I called her to ask her what she would do if she were me. I texted a local friend. Both of them offered to pitch in for us to get him a crate. I considered continuing the fundraising route since there were now three of us who could pitch in and then I saw that someone had responded to my post on Next Door.

It just said "Call me," with a name and phone number.

My old conditioned skeptic mind immediately thought, *this might be a scammer*, but I remembered the mission and decided not to roadblock myself. If it turned out the person was a scammy freak I could always block the number. I looked at the photo and it showed a picture of a lady with a dog, so I took comfort in knowing I was dealing with another animal lover.

I called and it immediately went to voicemail, but the woman sounded legit. Her name was Linda.

Linda called me back. I answered.

"I'm at the nail salon right now in Palm Harbor but I'm right down the way from a Petco and can go shopping after. I'm on the board of the VFWA and can probably file a claim and get reimbursed. If not, it's no biggie. How big is the dog?"

She loved dogs AND Veterans and just so happened to see my post. Wow. Earth Angels do exist. I unexpectedly burst into tears.

I explained that he broke through a heavy-duty crate. I sent her the pictures. She found the same crate on Amazon and sent me a screenshot. She ordered the crate but said it could not be delivered until the following week. She said she would head to the Petco to get him something temporary in the meantime. We chatted one more time, I gave her the address, and we agreed to meet up approximately 20 minutes later at the Veteran's house.

We pulled up at the exact same time. She had the crate in a box and we carried it in together. She had also picked up a bag with two large doggie tennis balls for Bandit.

The sweet Veteran met us at the door and he was in tears.

He looked at me. "Why are you doing this? I just really need to know."

I kind of wondered why he was asking me this and not Linda and then it occurred to me that if it were not for me, there wouldn't be a Linda in the story.

"Because I have a dog that I love. And I couldn't imagine giving her up. I'm an Empath. And you need that dog in your life." I said.

Linda chimed in that she had four dogs and doesn't even like it when one of them leaves the room. We all laughed.

She gave the bag of balls to Bandit and he tore into it, growling and playing with one of them.

We said goodbye to the Veteran and went outside. I showed her my necklace with the 444 that I got for Christmas from a friend. I told her it means you are surrounded by angels. She gasped and asked me if she could take a picture of it. She then told me a story about her nephew. He died of a rare blood cancer and his football number was 44 so whenever her family sees repeating fours they take photos and say, "Guess who was around today?" I loved it that Linda, like me, believed in the spirit world.

I was legit blown away that there are so many Angels among us. Linda and Bandit being two of them, and I, myself, having the opportunity to be one also.

It was also a lesson in how powerful we are once we have decided to go after something we need or want, whether for ourselves or someone else.

Intention + Inspired Action = MIRACLES.

Don't ever stop believing.

There are no coincidences, only synchronicities.

NEAR DEATH EXPERIENCE #1

So, I'd like to thank God, Angels, Universe, Spirit Guides and my intuition for sparing me in this particular close call. The close call that propelled me to re-evaluate how much of my time and energy I was giving to Corporate America.

I was working as a Territory Sales Trainer for a plastic surgery company that did facelifts and the like back in 2013. There was an unexpected incident that year during the month of September in the Nashville location. A patient had died on the operating table. The staff was very shaken by the incident, and my operations partner suggested we go there to support them. Because it was a last-minute decision, I made the choice to drive instead of fly. I rented a car for the trip.

It was the day after Labor Day. I was getting close to my destination and decided to give a few of my family members a call to let them know of my whereabouts. I got into a lengthy conversation with my Aunt, completely missed an exit, and drove about 20 miles out of my way in the wrong direction. Once I realized this, I got off the phone and pulled over at a local gas station in what felt like the middle of nowhere. I walked inside to use the bathroom. I bought an iced tea. The place sold fried chicken and some rough looking pizza. I got back in the car with the intent of getting back on the highway in the right direction.

I went to make a left turn to pull out on the access road and get back on the highway, however, there was a big silver tank truck to my left which was completely obstructing my view. I made an assessment of the place again; it felt like it was in the middle of nowhere and everything was super quiet. I hesitated because I could not see if there were any cars coming from the left. I waited for about 30 seconds. No cars coming my way. The silver trailer and my car were the only vehicles at the station. I picked up my foot to put it on the gas pedal to pull out and turn left on what appeared to be a deserted road. As I went to touch my foot to the gas pedal, I heard, what seemed like out loud but may have just been in my head, the word "NO."

I put my foot back on the brake. At that exact moment a blue sports car whizzed by in front of me. It had to have been going at least 60 miles an hour. My heart began to pound. I put the car back into park and just sat there, panting. Realizing how lucky I was to be alive. If I had made that left turn, that car would have slammed into my driver door and I would have been a goner. And I knew it.

The silver tank truck slowly turned left and got back on the highway. I watched it leave like it was happening in slow motion. I thank God that I didn't hit the gas and try to turn left. There would likely be no me if I had. I proceeded to the surgery center and talked with the staff. Turned out there was really no negligence on the part of the surgeon doing the procedure where the woman died. We talked about the fact that maybe it was just "her time" to go.

That night, back at the hotel, I had a "Come to Jesus" meeting with myself. How crazy that I was somewhere where I wasn't even supposed to be because of my absent-mindedness, and the fact that I truly felt like I had cheated death. It got me thinking about how handing over the boundless commitment and energy to a company that could let me go tomorrow was displaced loyalty. I wasn't wrong. The company did wind up doing some "corporate cutbacks" the very next month and my position was eliminated.

To this day, I have no idea how the "No" message I received in that split second was the thing that saved me from what would have no doubt been a fatal accident. I was grateful for knowing it wasn't "my time" to go.

So, interesting segue here. I happened to be telling someone this story in December of 2024. I described it as a "near death" experience. My guides must have had a laugh, because I experienced a different kind of "near death" experience less than a week later. Read on.

NEAR DEATH EXPERIENCE #2

"None of us are promised tomorrow."

One minute you're enjoying a salmon dinner at a networking event. The next minute you pass out and fall off a stool. Face down on the floor with your butt in the air. Next thing you know, you're in an ambulance singing songs from *Grease* with a couple of super cute EMT's. Bear with me. This is a wacky story. I've been questioning whether or not I wanted to write about it and share it publicly but as my Mom reminded me recently, "Everything is Copy." (Thanks Nora Ephron.) On a Thursday evening in December of 2024, I fainted at an event. I don't typically faint. It's not a thing. I noticed I was feeling a little off after the dinner and presentation. I discreetly stepped outside to get some air. I considered telling the person I rode with that we should get going but I knew she was wrapping up, so I went back in and sat on a stool then apparently passed out and fell forward smack on my knees and forehead. The people who watched it said they thought I had broken my nose. I'm surprised my teeth are intact.

I came back to consciousness with several people leaning over me, asking me if I had seizures. They called 911 then tried to cancel the call once I was conscious again. Those EMT's don't play. If you call 911, they are coming. It's actually a blessing that they did. This was the closest I've ever come to a near death experience. My pulse was 40 beats per minute. My blood pressure was dangerously low. Just earlier that day, I had been on a sales call with a man who had lost two loved ones within two weeks. I had offered my condolences and literally said out loud to him that life was precious and that "none of us are promised tomorrow." I wholeheartedly believe this. It's one of the reasons I live with such gusto and dolphin energy, cuz you really never know when it's gonna be your time. With the EMT's gathered around me I felt like I was losing consciousness again. My vision went dark and all I could see were the hands of the EMT's in front of me. They were wearing gloves and the white gloves looked like they were glowing in the dark. It was like watching a crazy glow-in-the-dark Sci-Fi movie. It occurred to me in this moment that I could actually slip away. I didn't really feel altogether ready for that sort of thing but the thought hit me like a ton of bricks. Being an Intuitive, I realized how real it was. I started trying to compose some last words. I started to speak. "If I go, please tell my people….." I didn't finish the sentence. It seemed like no one was listening to me and I remember feeling frustrated and annoyed. I'm not really sure what I was trying to articulate anyway and hadn't defined who "my people" were. Funny how I always want the last word, even in an emergency. I got popped onto a stretcher and carried out to the ambulance. On the ride over, one of the EMT's was checking in with me. "What county are we in?"

"Pinellas," I said.

"What year is it?"

"2024"

"Who is the President Elect?"

"Donald J. Trump," I said confidently. "Impressive," said the EMT.

As we were riding I heard them say I was a 45-year-old woman more than once. Someone at the event probably was guessing my age on the 911 call. I spoke up. "I'm really flattered that you think I'm 45," I said. "I'm in my 50's." "That's okay. I'm just hitting on you," He joked. "It's okay," I said. "Everybody does." A quick reference here back to *Leading With Light Volume 1*, where I shared my ageless secret of imagining that everyone is ALWAYS hitting on me. I swear because of this I always have a much better time.

Pretty sure he didn't get the joke, but whatever. "Spell your last name," he says. I spell it for him. "Reidell?" He says "Like the high school in *Grease*?" Exactly, I say. Next thing I know he starts singing "Summer Loving" and I join in. Then I pulled out my favorite, "Hopelessly Devoted to You." Something was really comforting about singing it. It's one of my Karaoke favs but I can no longer hit the high notes. "Wow," says the EMT. "You've got quite the voice." I thank him. We got to the hospital. Dave was waiting in front of the ambulance door and started dancing to make me laugh. It worked. We were there until 2:30. Two CAT scans, three bags of fluid, and countless blood tests later I was released. Slight dehydration. No sign of heart trouble. No evidence of blood clots. I'm pretty sure I know what caused the pressure drop. Earlier that day I had a few vitamin injections and a shot of CoQ10 with the intended result being lowered blood pressure. Looks like it lowered my blood pressure all too well.

I still worked the next day and did some bang up sales calls. I wasn't going to let this incident get in the way of my income and my fun weekend plans. Screw that! I had a Golf Cart parade and an Ugly Sweater boat party on Sunday with my friends. It was time to get busy living again. Because that's what I do. I told Dave and my friends that if for some reason I had passed on I would have still wanted them to do the parade. They already knew that. I pondered whether they would have still done it or not. Plus, I had that audition on Saturday. I wasn't gonna miss it. (Spoiler alert-I got the part.) I talked to my Mom and told her the story. She listened in awe. "You SURE ARE living your Life Motto Baby Girl!" she exclaimed enthusiastically. She had said the exact same thing during Hurricane Milton when I texted her a photo having dinner and drinks with friends right before the Hurricane tore through Tampa in October. That's right. That life motto guides every last aspect of my life. Once I stopped judging myself for living into it things have REALLY gotten good. "I'll always have a great time NO MATTER WHAT." Even in the ER I kept trying to come up with ways to make the experience more fun. Admittedly, I fell a little short. My phone was in Dave's truck for the duration of the night which was probably for the best. At one point, he crammed himself into the hospital bed next to me and started snoring loudly. If I had my phone I would have recorded it for a future practical joke. "You should be resting!" one of my friends said to me that weekend. Maybe... but nah. I do know that at least 80% of the things we worry about never actually happen so I'm not going to take a time out waiting for the other shoe to drop when I feel fine.

I saw my General Practitioner a few days following the "incident" as I am calling it. I told him my theory about the CoQ10 shot. He actually agreed with me. I felt so seen. Over the past week, the words kept echoing like a gong in my head.

"None of us are promised TOMORROW."

That's why it's SO important to keep on living your absolute best life TODAY.

So, in conclusion, do me a favor. Please don't ever forget, there are no Coincidences, only Synchronicities.

Schedule an intuitive breakthrough session:

https://calendly.com/jess-33/intuitive-breakthrough-session-1

Phoenix Rayne

Phoenix is a licensed massage therapist-energy healer specializing in Quantum Touch and emotional energy release breath work, with passion and grace. Rising from her transformative journey, she empowers others to reclaim their inner light and heal from within. In her chapter, Phoenix shares her deep personal experience to inspire growth and self-empowerment. Her work invites others to explore deep healing and discover the power of aligning mind, body, and spirit.

If you're ready to embrace your own transformative healing journey, I invite you to connect with me for a complimentary session. Schedule a call through my Calendly link, and let's begin your path to healing together.

One Breath Away From Who You're Meant To Be

By Phoenix Rayne

RISING FROM THE ASHES: MY JOURNEY THROUGH LOSS, ADDICTION, AND AWAKENING

The journey of healing is never linear, nor is it predictable. Mine began with unimaginable loss—the kind that breaks you in ways you didn't know were possible—and took me through years of deep soul-searching, heartbreak, and ultimately, a profound spiritual awakening.

ETHAN'S ARRIVAL AND THE LOVE THAT CHANGED EVERYTHING

Ethan, my firstborn, came into this world showing me from day one that life is precious, fragile, and full of miracles. I still remember the complications leading up to his birth, how he was breech, and how his tiny foot kicked its way through my uterus. In a rush of panic, I was taken in for an emergency C-section. I didn't get to see him right away, but the moment they placed him in my arms, I felt an expansion in my heart like nothing I had ever experienced. It was as though my heart grew a size bigger in that instant, making room for a love so deep I could hardly comprehend it.

I can still picture his little lips quivering when he cried, how his tiny hands curled around my finger. From that moment on, I was a mother. Everything I thought I knew about life and love shifted to make space for this new reality. Ethan would be the child who taught me how to love unconditionally, who gave me a reason to wake up every morning with gratitude in my heart—no matter what challenges came our way.

GROWING PAINS AND EARLY STRUGGLES

Though motherhood changed me profoundly, life was never perfectly smooth. I had my share of challenges. I experienced traumas and heartbreaks growing up that shaped me in ways I didn't fully understand. Over the years, I struggled with self-esteem, never quite feeling that I was enough. I carried wounds from my past into my adult life, and sometimes, those wounds bled into my ability to be fully present for my children.

Still, I tried my best. I believed in love, in the goodness of people, and in the hope that tomorrow could be better than today. Yet, these beliefs were often overshadowed by fear and an undercurrent of unresolved pain. That pain made me vulnerable, and I eventually turned to substances for a sense of relief. What began as a coping mechanism gradually became an addiction, a desperate attempt to numb the wounds I didn't know how to heal.

A SLOWLY EVOLVING ADDICTION

Addiction, for me, was a gradual, insidious process. At first, it was just a way to take the edge off—painkillers or something stronger when life felt unbearable. But as time went on, I sank deeper and deeper. I would have spurts of sobriety, periods of time when I believed I was finally in control. But life's challenges—financial stress, relational issues, unresolved trauma—would come crashing back in, and I found myself chasing that numbness again.

Despite my struggles, I always had a glimmer of faith inside me that believed things would work out. Maybe it was naive. Maybe it was the mother in me who desperately wanted to hold onto hope. Maybe it was a quiet voice of spirit, whispering that I wasn't alone. Regardless, that spark of faith, though dim at times, never fully died out, even in my darkest moments.

MY SISTER'S MOVE TO COLORADO

By the time 2020 arrived, the world was reeling from the COVID-19 pandemic, and I was already living in a form of isolation that felt harsher than any lockdown. I was living out of motels in Colorado, deeply entrenched in my addiction. My sister, who had recently moved to Colorado herself, knew I was struggling. We didn't see each other as often as sisters normally would; addiction has a way of separating you from everyone who cares about you, either through shame or the chaotic lifestyle you start to live.

Even so, she reached out to me on Christmas of that year. I was in such a haze that I barely questioned why she wanted to spend Christmas with me, especially since she had her own children and family obligations. Part of me was simply relieved that someone cared enough to want my presence. Another part of me was so numb that I couldn't feel the heaviness brewing beneath the surface.

CHRISTMAS 2020: THE NIGHT MY WORLD SHATTERED

When my sister picked me up on Christmas Day, I could sense her unease, but I pushed aside any suspicions. We arrived at a hotel, and I remember her dog, an Australian Shepherd named Sadie, padding around the room while we settled in. The atmosphere felt tense, and I finally asked, "What's wrong? You're scaring me."

I'll never forget the look on my sister's face. It was like she carried the weight of the world in her eyes. Then she told me the words that still echo in my mind: "They found Ethan's body. He's gone. He was shot and killed."

It's impossible to describe the moment your entire reality disintegrates in front of you. I collapsed to the floor, screaming, sobbing, pleading for this not to be true. My sweet baby boy—the reason I first knew true, unconditional love—was gone. All the oxygen seemed to leave my lungs, and I thought I might die right there from the agony. In that instant, I understood that life could change so irrevocably in a single breath.

DESCENT INTO DESPAIR

In the hours that followed, I went on autopilot. I still had drugs on me, and I used them to escape the unbearable onslaught of emotions. My sister called my aunt, and they discussed ways to help me. That night, I was presented with a choice: stay in Colorado and likely die from my grief and addiction, or move to Florida, where my ex-husband and my two younger children lived, and try to build a new life.

Though I could barely think straight, I knew deep down that I had to choose life—for my other children's sake if not for my own. The next day, my sister took me to the motel where I had been staying so I could collect my things. I grabbed what I could, hiding some drugs in my bag because I feared the looming withdrawals. She then dropped me at the airport. I boarded a plane in a daze, my heart in a million pieces, my body already protesting the lack of chemicals it had come to depend on.

FLORIDA: THE FIRST STEPS INTO RECOVERY

Arriving in Florida was surreal. My ex-husband, who had been sober for a few years, welcomed me, as did my children. They were trying to be strong for me, but I sensed their worry and their own grief for the brother they'd lost. Within a few days, I was in the throes of withdrawal, lying in bed, wracked with chills, body aches, and an ache in my soul that felt even deeper.

Eventually, I began Suboxone to manage the worst of the withdrawal symptoms. Physically, I started to stabilize after about a week, though emotionally, I was still a wreck. My sister, who had shown me more compassion and love than I felt I deserved, arranged a celebration of life for Ethan in Texas. She found a beautiful Airbnb by the lake; a place she believed Ethan would have loved.

ETHAN'S CELEBRATION OF LIFE

In mid-January, we flew to Texas for the memorial. Family, friends, and acquaintances came to pay their respects to my son. The heartbreak was overwhelming, and I found myself drinking to cope. I wasn't yet ready to embrace sobriety fully; the pain of losing Ethan felt too massive to face without some form of self-medication. But even in my haze, I recognized this event as a turning point. My sister again took the reins, handling all the logistics with grace and compassion. I clung to her strength because I had none of my own.

During that time, my aunt told me about a spiritual teacher she'd been working with and encouraged me to explore a healing modality called Quantum Touch energy healing. I didn't grasp its significance immediately, but the idea planted a small seed of hope in my mind—maybe there was something out there that could help me heal not just from addiction, but from the immense grief consuming me.

A MYSTERIOUS OWL AND A BREWING AWAKENING

Looking back, I believe the universe was sending me signs even before Ethan's death. A few weeks prior, I was outside my hotel in Boulder, Colorado, when a white owl flew overhead. This owl circled above me, hooting insistently, seemingly unafraid of my friend's dog. It felt like it was trying to communicate something, and I remember standing there in awe. At first, I thought it might be my father, who had passed away about a month before Ethan's murder. But after losing Ethan, I wondered if it was a messenger from the spirit world, a guide preparing me for the unimaginable upheaval that was about to enter my life.

Whatever the owl represented, it remained a powerful symbol. Part of me questioned the idea of a mystical sign, but another part felt oddly comforted—like there was a realm of understanding just beyond my reach, waiting for me to accept it.

ETHAN'S VISIT IN A DREAM

Not long after he died, Ethan came to me in a dream. This wasn't an ordinary dream, where things feel hazy or nonsensical. It was vivid, lucid. I saw him standing there, and I knew he was gone—yet there he was, whole and present. Though he didn't speak out loud, I heard his voice in my mind: Let it be. It's okay. I felt an overwhelming sense of peace emanating from him. It was as if he wanted me to know that he was fine, that I didn't need to cling so tightly to the horror and the pain.

That dream became a lifeline. Whenever my grief threatened to pull me under, I recalled his words and his presence. It didn't erase the pain, but it gave me hope that maybe his spirit lived on in some way, and that maybe I could live on, too.

Returning to Florida after the memorial, I desperately needed some semblance of normalcy. Still reeling from my son's death, I knew I had to start piecing myself together, however slowly.

QUANTUM TOUCH, MEDITATION, AND A NEW JOB

I took a leap of faith and decided to pursue new avenues of healing. My aunt had mentioned Quantum Touch energy healing to me around the time of Ethan's memorial, and her encouragement kept echoing in my mind. Eventually, I signed up for courses and started immersing myself in the world of energy healing, practicing techniques that would help me release the deep, unprocessed grief stuck in my body.

After living in Florida for some time I eventually reconnected with my background in massage therapy, finding a job at a local spa. It was a crucial step in reclaiming some sense of normalcy and responsibility. By day, I offered healing touch to clients, and by night, I delved into meditation and further energy-work practices. Oddly enough, even though I was still wrestling with the loss of my son, I found solace in helping others feel better—physically, mentally, and energetically.

Looking back, I believe this year laid the foundation for my eventual recovery. I was still on Suboxone, still grappling with addiction's shadows, but the seeds of transformation were being planted through my exploration of Quantum Touch, meditation, and the daily act of showing up for work. It was like learning to breathe again after having the wind knocked out of me.

A PROPOSAL AND LINGERING UNCERTAINTY

By the summer of 2021, I had been living in Florida for several months. My ex-husband, seeing my progress and wanting to support me, asked me to marry him again. I was overwhelmed with gratitude for the kindness he had shown me—welcoming me into his home when I was at rock bottom. In my confusion and lingering grief, I said yes, partly because it felt like the "right thing" to do. I hoped this step might bring stability and help me move forward.

Yet beneath the surface, I wasn't sure I was ready. I had just begun discovering my own strength and spirituality. Grief can leave you disoriented, and while I loved him for his support, I also felt uncertain about who I was without substances or external validation. The proposal was a bright spot in a dark year, but it also highlighted the unanswered questions that still haunted me: *Who am I, really? What do I want my life to look like now that Ethan is gone?*

SUMMER 2022: REHAB, GETTING OFF SUBOXONE, AND TRIPLE RELAPSE

Although I'd managed to hold things together for most of 2021, by summer of 2022, I knew I needed a more decisive step toward true sobriety. I had been on Suboxone for a while, but I didn't feel fully alive. With my husband's encouragement, I entered rehab to finally come off Suboxone and tackle the underlying addiction issues that still lurked within me.

Rehab was an intense experience. I faced the guilt, shame, and grief I'd been numbing for so long. When I got out, however, I quickly discovered how unprepared I was to handle raw life on life's terms. I relapsed three times in succession, each slip filling me with a paralyzing sense of failure and despair. Still, each relapse taught me something valuable about my triggers and my internal wounds.

During these tumultuous months, I also became more involved in the 12 Steps. I started working more in depth with my sponsor, began attending meetings regularly, and started to actually work the Steps in earnest. My last relapse, May 5, 2023 was my breaking point—the moment when I truly surrendered to the process. Though I achieved sobriety, I continued to struggle with deep depression.

BINGE-WATCHING, DEPRESSION, AND THE DARK NIGHT OF THE SOUL

I was free from substances but wrestling with what felt like an endless dark night of the soul. I fell into periods of deep depression, often spending my days when I wasn't at work, or when I got off of work glued to my screen, binge-watching shows just to escape my thoughts. Grief over Ethan's death still weighed heavily on me, and the reality of living without the crutches of heroin or Suboxone was more challenging than I ever imagined.

Despite my involvement in recovery groups, I couldn't shake the sense of emptiness. My meditations and energy practices were not being done. I questioned everything—my marriage, my beliefs, my purpose. Looking back, I realize this phase was a painfully necessary purging of old identities and patterns. It was a crucible in which my spirit was being refined, although it felt like I was being reduced to ashes day after day.

2024: A STIRRING OF HOPE AND THE EMOTIONAL ENERGY RELEASE INVITATION

When 2024 arrived, something in me shifted. After months of depression, I sensed a quiet stirring, a call to break free from the malaise I'd fallen into. I remember having a distinct moment of clarity: I cannot live like this anymore. I needed a different path, a new way to process all the trauma, grief, and confusion that had accumulated over the past few years.

Right around this time, I received a text about a training for Emotional Energy Release Breathwork. As well as finally saying yes to starting the course I began in July 2024 for Quantum Leap Intensive Coaching, something I had been feeling guided to do for quite some time. The timing felt too perfect to be coincidence, as though my higher power was placing an opportunity right in front of me. Despite lingering doubts, I signed up for both courses, hoping it would help me dig deeper into the emotional blocks that were still holding me hostage.

Simultaneously, I knew I needed space to truly explore who I was—apart from being someone's wife, someone's mother, or someone in recovery. As much as I loved my husband for all he had done, I felt I was losing myself in our dynamic. By the summer of 2024, I made the difficult decision to move out, enrolling in sober living and immersing myself in this new breathwork training and coaching course. It was one of the hardest moves I've ever made, yet I sensed it was a necessary step toward self-discovery and genuine independence.

ETHAN'S MEMORY AND THE SEEDS OF AWAKENING

Throughout this entire timeline, my son Ethan remained my anchor and my inspiration. Even in my most drug-addled haze, or in the darkest throes of depression, I carried with me the dream in which he appeared, telling me, "Let it be. It's okay." I held onto the memory of his quivering lips when he cried as a newborn, the way he first taught me about unconditional love. Although losing him was the catalyst for so much suffering, it was also the spark that propelled me toward recovery, spirituality, and healing practices I never would have explored otherwise.

I often reflected on the signs and synchronicities around his death—like the white owl that hovered above me in Colorado shortly before Ethan's murder, as if warning me of a coming storm. Or the books on energy healing and soul contracts that seemed to appear at exactly the right moments. These events reassured me that there was a greater tapestry at work, weaving together pain, growth, and divine guidance in ways I was only beginning to understand.

WORKING THE 12 STEPS, EXPLORING ENERGY WORK, AND FINDING MY VOICE

From 2021 to 2024, I delved into multiple healing modalities, drawing upon them with increasing focus as the years passed. Quantum Touch became a cornerstone, showing me how energy flows beyond physical boundaries and how much power we have to heal through our higher power. My training in Emotional Energy Release Breathwork opened the door to deeper emotional processing—allowing me to release pent-up anger, grief, and shame in a controlled, supportive environment.

Meanwhile, the 12 Steps gave me a sense of community and accountability that I desperately needed. I learned to name my resentments, make amends for my part in the chaos, and embrace a higher power of my own understanding. Rather than feeling forced into a predefined notion of "God," I discovered a loving, guiding presence that I could trust with my pain and my future.

Little by little, I started to uncover who I really was beneath the layers of trauma, addiction, and societal programming. I realized I had a gift for holding space for others in their darkest moments. My experiences—homelessness, heartbreak, losing a child—became not just scars but badges of empathy. I could understand suffering in a way that allowed me to connect with people on a soul level.

HONORING MY SON AND EMBRACING MY PURPOSE

Although I still grieve Ethan's absence every day, I've made the conscious choice to honor his memory by fully living my own life. As I steadily grow stronger—physically, emotionally, and spiritually—I feel closer to him, as though we're still walking side by side. His presence is woven through my work in energy healing, my new understanding of soul contracts, and my desire to help others transform their pain into purpose.

The more I've learned, the more I believe our lives are woven with intricate plans, or at least possibilities, that we choose before we're born. Perhaps Ethan and I had a sacred contract, agreeing to learn from each other in both life and death. Whether or not this is verifiable truth, it gives me peace, reminding me that our bond is unbreakable.

CONCLUSION: A LIFE REBUILT, A SOUL RENEWED

As I look back, I see a story of resilience, even though it's been peppered with setbacks and heartbreak. From a homeless addict in Colorado to a committed energy healer and breathwork coach in Florida, my trajectory has often felt like riding stormy seas without a compass. Yet each trial—Ethan's death, addiction relapses, painful goodbyes—was also a catalyst that drew me toward deeper healing and understanding.

Today, I continue to walk this path, aware that healing is a lifelong process. I still face challenges and lingering shadows of depression, but I greet them with greater self-compassion and spiritual insight. My sobriety, which finally took root after repeated relapses, is something I cherish—and protect—because it allows me to be fully present for my children, for my clients, and for the memory of Ethan.

My story is not merely about surviving tragedy; it's about discovering the power of love, surrender, and spiritual connection. I share these words in the hope that anyone reading who feels lost or broken might see a reflection of their own potential. We each carry within us the seeds of renewal, the capacity to rise from the darkest depths. May my path serve as one small light on your own journey, reminding you that even after unimaginable loss, a new life—and a deeper sense of purpose—can emerge.

SYNOPSIS

Homeless and immersed in the grip of addiction, the author faces the unimaginable tragedy of her first-born son, Ethan, being murdered. Struggling with grief and despair, she is nonetheless guided toward a path of recovery- sparked by family support, signs from Ethan, and a growing spiritual awareness. Through rehab, the 12 steps, and the discovery of energy healing practices, she gradually reclaims her life, forging a profound connection to her higher power and her own inner strength. With Ethan's memory as her compass, she transforms her pain into purpose, ultimately finding hope, healing, and a renewed commitment to helping others break free from the cycle of trauma and addiction.

BIO

Phoenix is a mother of three, a certified Breathwork Coach, Quantum Touch Practitioner, Prosperity Energy Healing Guided Meditation Hypnosis, LMT, and Transformational mentor who turned her own profound grief into a guiding light for others. After experiencing the heartbreaking loss of her son, Phoenix found solace and empowerment through holistic healing methods, alongside therapy-most notably breathwork and energy work. Through her personal journey, she discovered her calling: to help people release emotional blockages, uncover hidden resilience, and embrace a life of purpose.

Today Phoenix draws on her lived experience and professional training to guide clients toward self-love, spiritual growth, and deep inner healing. Whether through guided meditation groups, one-on-one, or written work, Phoenix's heartfelt mission remains the same: to inspire others to transform their pain into power and step into the limitless potential of a life well-lived.

Connect with Phoenix for a free consultation: **https://calendly. com/iamjessmathis3/30min**

Leigh Hamilton

Out of the Shadows, Into the Light

By Leigh Hamilton

This is my story of how I came to understand that the darkness I was in was merely the shadow I had cast from the way I approached life.

Once I shifted how I saw myself, the world and life, I was then able to see the light that surrounded me.

I grew up in a loving family with two parents who were heavily involved in my childhood. My mum was on committees at the school and local soccer club and my dad coached soccer for a few years. Mum stayed at home with my sister and me, whilst my dad worked to provide for us. Dad would always get out in the backyard to muck around with mum occasionally joining in as well.

Why do I tell you this?

For as long as I can remember, growing up, I was never a confident kid, somewhat quiet and shy. I always doubted my abilities and what I was capable of, and as I got older these feelings only intensified inside of me. It didn't matter what anyone said, I didn't believe them.

One thing that stopped me from overcoming these feelings was that everywhere, in everything I read, it said that a lack of confidence, no self-belief all stems from a childhood trauma. But I didn't go through any childhood trauma. I had two loving parents that always looked out for me. So, I felt embarrassed and ashamed that I was feeling this way for no apparent reason. I just pushed it down inside, put on a mask to the outside world, and kept going. I buried those feelings inside and wouldn't show anyone how I was truly feeling in fear of judgment because I didn't fit the mold of what someone feeling this way should be.

Like a lot of men, I got an apprenticeship, managed to get a good job in the mines, and managed to buy a house for myself and my young family. I had all the things that should have made me happy with life. For moments intime, I did experience happiness, but it was always surface level, deep down I never felt happy. Again, people would say to me, "You should be happy, look at what you have." And whilst their intentions were good, that made me feel worse because I could see what I had but I wasn't happy internally. So, I'd agree and continue to bury how I really felt deep down inside, too embarrassed to talk about how I was really feeling.

Then came October 2011. I sat in the Doctor's office and he said to me, "You have Ulcerative Colitis (think painful food poisoning 24/7). We don't know what causes it but we do know it's hereditary. There is no known cure for it. You will have to take medication for the rest of your life."

To say I was devastated was an understatement. I was already struggling with life, now I had to deal with this incurable disease. And honestly, I didn't deal with it. Once again I internalized everything and didn't show how I was really feeling to anyone, and this I believe is part of what cost me my relationship with my partner at the time. I was so embarrassed and ashamed by everything that I was going through that I just shut down how I was feeling and kept everyone at a distance. Like a lot of people out there, whenever I was around people, I would disguise how I was feeling with humor and wit. I never went looking to be the center of attention but if the people I was with were being cheeky and smart arses, then I was able to hold my own with the best of them, all whilst hiding how unhappy I was.

I was living a life constantly stressed and anxious about what others thought of me. Is my Colitis going to play up, what will others think if I suddenly have to run off to the toilet (how embarrassing will that be), what sort of a father am I, constantly feeling sick and unable to get out and kick the soccer ball with my son, and the list goes on. Which led to thoughts of, why is this happening to me, what have I done to deserve this, why can't I catch a break.

Avoiding how I felt, both mentally and physically, led me to having anxiety attacks. In 2017, one morning I woke up, had a shower, got dressed and then as I was about to leave to go to work, I dropped to the ground and started shaking, unable to get up and go to work. This lasted for –three to four weeks. That was my darkest time. I kept the roller shutters down, the curtains closed, the front door shut. I didn't want anything from the outside world coming in. I wanted to hide away from everything and everyone.

What kept me going was the thought of my kids, and not wanting to leave them without a father. No matter what, I was always going to be there for my kids.

That was when I made the choice to change. I didn't know what or how, I just knew I had to. I didn't want my kids to have to go through this, so, I knew I had to not only teach them a better way, but show them as well. I was still embarrassed and ashamed by what was happening, so talking to someone didn't feel like an option. I turned to YouTube and spent hours upon hours watching different videos. Some useful, some not so useful. I also started to read self-help books. Some things I read in the books I was able to grasp immediately, other things took a while for me to grasp because I didn't understand what was written and the same with the YouTube videos. As I was embarrassed and ashamed to talk to anyone, I didn't discuss it with anyone to gain an understanding.

This meant it took me longer than it should have to learn some of these concepts.

This is a big reason why I stepped into being a coach, so that I could provide both a safe space for people to talk, judgment free, but also give people someone to talk to so they can gain a better understanding on why we do some things and how to move forward and overcome them.

So, how did I get from where I was to where I am today, here sharing my story with you?

I decided that I was no longer just going to exist in this life, but that I was actually going to start living. There were two reasons for this, the first and biggest reason was my kids. I didn't want them to grow up and experience what I was going through. I knew I had to show them a different way of living.

The second was the fear of what other people were thinking of me. This was a double-edged sword, because part of me feared judgment and caused a lot of anxiety. But without realizing it at the time, that fear also drove me to change. Because of the fear of people judging me for being the way I was, drove me to want to be different.

With this pain, fear, and wanting to be different, I committed to changing. I didn't know how, I just committed to it. And funnily enough, as I made this decision, different things started to appear in my life to help me along the way.

The first thing that hit me was my thoughts when left to themselves, they are not my friends. They will do everything they can to keep me in my "comfort zone", in a place of familiarity, even if that place is painful or bad. My thoughts, my mind, does not like the unknown.

So, for most of us our minds and thoughts keep talking "negatively," which in return turns our focus onto the "negative" things in our lives, and then we miss all the "positive" that happens. And believe me, it happens a lot more than we realize.

I realized that I had handed over control of who I was and how I felt to my thoughts and mind. They didn't want to see me thrive (because it was an unknown place for me), but wanted to keep me "safe" despite "safe" being damaging to both my mental and physical health.

With this new understanding of my thoughts and mind, I decided that I would now take control of the wheel and start driving my own life. This led my focus and attention inwards on who I was and how I reacted to life when things happened around me. I learnt what things triggered me and what things I loved, where I felt comfortable and where I felt uncomfortable.

For the first time, I had an understanding of who I was. And I'll be honest, some of the things I learnt about myself weren't good. A part of me was ashamed by how I had acted in the past, and this weighed me down again. Seeing those things from my past started to bring up my old way of thinking, and with no one to help keep me moving forward, there was a moment I felt myself start to slip into old habits. But after some time, I realized that now I had a starting point, now I had a choice to continue to be and act the way I always have or I could change those things and start to show up differently.

Like the cliche saying goes "1% better every day". Given my actions up until now had me living a life with illness, anxiety, and depression, I made the decision to change.

Ok, great, I see the things in myself I no longer want to be, fantastic, I'll just do the opposite, or so I thought. I thought just doing the opposite would make me happy and confident. It didn't quite work that way.

While I had decided on who I didn't want to be, I hadn't decided on who I wanted to be. While at face value these two statements may seem the same, when you delve deeper they are quite different. I realized that it was up to me to decide on what type of person I wanted to be. It was quite daunting at first, when you've lived for so long being molded by the outside world, but it was also exhilarating at the same time, because now I got to choose and decide for myself who I wanted to be.

This took some time, as I thought about how do I want to show up for my kids, as a son, a partner, a friend and to the world. How do I want to show up every day?

Once I decided on who I wanted to be and how I wanted to show up, I set out to learn how to gain these attributes and skills. I wanted the steps to be that way. But everywhere I looked I was hearing, "You have to start being that way." This didn't sit well with me. My anxiety went through the roof. Those old "negative" thoughts came back.

"I don't know how to do that. What if I get it wrong? What if I get laughed at? What if I fail?"

I started to feel stuck again, old thought patterns started to slowly creep back in.

The thought of being something different when my perception was that I didn't know how to be that way was daunting. I hadn't learnt anything to suggest I knew how to change. Then I stopped over-thinking it and thought, what does each attribute mean to me and if I think about myself with that attribute how am I showing up? That's when I could see that I in fact did know myself and it was just a matter of presenting myself that way. Some days this was easier than others, and some attributes were easier to embody than others as well.

Embracing new attributes and characteristics is something that I find I continue to do over time as I learn more and more about who I am. And one thing that I have noticed is that having someone there to help keep you moving forward always made it easier to embrace the new attribute quicker.

With this newfound understanding of myself and how I now started to feel comfortable with who I am, I realized that whenever something in my life, either a situation or someone saying or doing something, I found I was still emotionally affected by it. I would still overthink it and let it bring me down and back to judging myself harshly. And although the darkness from these situations wouldn't last the weeks or months they would have in the past they would still last a day or two and they were still quite heavy emotions to feel.

I came to understand that just like in order to be comfortable with who I am I have to accept myself, in order for me to not be so affected by the external world. I have to accept others and situations for who and what they are. Sounded simple enough initially until I tried to embrace this new way of thinking. I found that because I was emotionally affected by what was happening, it was difficult to just accept and let go. Part of me still felt "connected" or "linked" to what was happening. It was like I had a part to play in everything going on. So, if someone was having a bad day and they were short with me in a conversation, I would immediately think, What have I done wrong?

I was always quick to label any situation or experience as "Negative" or "Positive" which in turn would then affect me.

I learnt that any and all situations and experiences weren't "negative" or "positive," they were "neutral." It was me who was in fact labelling these experiences.

On December 7, 2021, I was made redundant from my job of 15 years. At this time, I struggled with both my mental and physical health. I was initially devastated by the news. I had no idea of how someone with Ulcerative Colitis in my condition would be able to find another job. For two weeks, I was scared and anxious about what I was going to do, and I was depressed by what had happened. Once again, with this big shift in my life, I felt lost.

But after two weeks I began to see this as a way to start following what I was passionate about. I'd always loved helping others when they'd come to me and open up and talk to me about their personal lives. Note, at this time though, I was an electrician, and it was not part of my role. People just felt comfortable to come talk to me.

At that moment, I decided that being made redundant was now an opportunity for me to step into something new. It was no longer a negative event, but now, in fact, a positive one. It was the start of a new journey towards the person I wanted to be, (a Life Coach).

I'm sure we've all had something happen that we initially thought was a negative experience which turned out to be a positive one. But it was only with hindsight that we realize that. So now, being aware of this, I made the choice to look at each experience and situation as an experience or situation. I didn't label them good or bad. This didn't necessarily mean that I agreed with the situation or experience, or was happy about it, but I accepted it.

It was the same with people, it was hard to accept when someone was rude or did something I didn't agree with or maybe even disrespected me. If this happened in the past, I would either think I had done something wrong or I'd spend hours or days angry or upset over what had happened. This would just lead to more stress in my life and then I would get anxious the next time I had to see that person.

But I came to understand that most people will only do what they believe is right for them and their family the same way I do. Again, this doesn't mean that I think what they are doing is right and I might not agree with it. But in their eyes they believe their actions and/or words are warranted.

Realizing this, I thought how can I judge someone else for doing what they believe is right, when I live my life the same way. This allowed me to accept what others say and do, even though I don't always agree with them.

Why am I writing this chapter? Well, for a few reasons. One is that while we all experience different situations in our lives, we all experience the same emotions and I want everyone to understand they are not alone in what they are feeling, despite what they see in the world around them. Knowing this can help us to feel less alienated in the world and give us strength to keep going.

My main reason is to help share with everyone what helped me find my way from the darkness into the light. To be that Shadow Warrior standing next to you as you fight your way through your own darkness. Sometimes all we need is that warrior beside us that gives us that added strength, courage, and confidence to keep fighting.

Remembering what it was like feeling trapped in the darkness and never wanting to feel that way again, as well as a deep desire to help others break free of their own darkness and find their own light is why I wrote this chapter and why I walked away from 20 years as an electrician and became a transformational coach.

Just because you feel trapped in the darkness now does not mean that's how it always needs to be. Let's fight together and find your way to your light.

Patsy Hobson & Rae Mitchell

Patsy and Rae are transformational coaches and co-creators of The Inner Peace Revolution, empowering women to rediscover inner peace, purpose, and joy. With decades of experience in self-development, they blend many modalities to create profound shifts. Their approach integrates mindset work, spiritual connection, and the wisdom of the Superconscious mind, guiding women to live in alignment with their true essence. Through The Inner Peace Revolution, they provide a nurturing space where women feel seen, heard, and supported. Their mission is to help women embrace their limitless potential and flow with the natural rhythm of life.

Rediscovering Inner Peace

A Journey of Rhythm and Transformation

By Patsy Hobson & Rae Mitchell

There comes a moment in every woman's life when the world around her falls silent, and for the first time in a long time, she can hear it, the quiet voice inside, the one she has pushed aside for years. **It's a whisper, a gentle yet persistent knowing: 'There has to be more than this.'** It's a whisper that often emerges in the stillness, perhaps in the early hours of the morning before the demands of the day descend, or in a fleeting moment of solitude that feels both foreign and precious. It's not a cry of despair but a call to awaken, to step into something more aligned, more meaningful, more you.

We've heard that whisper too. For years, we moved through life, ticking all the boxes society told us would lead to happiness and fulfillment. Careers, relationships, families, achievements, on the surface, it looked like we had it all together. But beneath that polished veneer, something felt off. There was a disconnect, a yearning for something deeper that no external success could satisfy.

For one of us, the breaking point came in a hospital room, depleted to the core after years of prioritising everyone else's needs while quietly ignoring her own. For the other, it was the collapse of a relationship she had fought desperately to fix, only to realise that the person who truly needed saving was herself.

These moments weren't the beginning of our journeys, they were the wake up calls that forced us to pause, reassess, and ultimately pivot toward a different way of being. But our stories aren't about those singular moments of crisis. They're about the patterns that led us there and the transformation that followed. They're about rediscovering the rhythms of life, those natural, fluid cycles that bring balance, vitality, and clarity. And they're about guiding others to do the same.

THE INNER PEACE REVOLUTION

This work became the foundation for what we now call *The Inner Peace Revolution*. It's not just a program; it's a movement to help women reclaim their power, reconnect with their inner peace, and live lives that feel aligned and fulfilling.

Through years of self-discovery, learning, and guiding others, we developed our signature framework: Initiate, Integrate, and Ignite. These three stages form the foundation of our approach to helping women move from chaos to peace.

- **INITIATE:** This is where the journey begins. It's about self-awareness, identifying the patterns that no longer serve you, and awakening to the possibilities of change. You might feel stuck, unsure why nothing is changing despite your efforts. You may be questioning your direction or feel disconnected from what once brought you joy. In this stage, we help you gain clarity on where you are in your life and where you truly want to go. We guide you in dropping into your heart space, where all the answers lie, and connecting with the innocence and wonder of life once again. Through reflective journaling, self-inquiry practices, and guided meditations, you'll uncover a deeper understanding of your desires and unlock the courage to move forward.
- **INTEGRATE:** Once awareness is gained, it's time to embody your newfound insights. This stage focuses on aligning your mind, body, and spirit to create harmony. You may notice old

stories playing on repeat, telling you that you're not enough, that you should be doing more, that slowing down is a luxury you can't afford. We explore how you perceive your life and others, helping you shift perspectives that may be holding you back. You'll learn to listen to your body's communication signals, recognising them as valuable guides to your well-being. Gratitude and forgiveness become powerful tools in this process, fostering a more positive outlook and opening the door to greater emotional resilience. Through daily practices, breathwork, and visualisation exercises, you will begin weaving sustainable rhythms into your everyday life.

- **IGNITE:** The final stage is about transformation, stepping into your power, embracing your authentic self, and living in alignment with your purpose. Here, we focus on uncovering your why and aligning your actions with what truly lights you up. Perhaps you've found yourself going through the motions, doing what's expected, keeping up with responsibilities, but feeling a growing sense that there's something more. Maybe it's a passion you've sidelined for years, or a dream you've convinced yourself is out of reach. Ignite is about giving yourself permission to claim those desires, to engage in activities that spark joy and fulfillment, and to step into your full potential. We support you in developing a vision that excites you and taking intentional action steps that keep you aligned with your purpose.

But transformation doesn't happen in isolation. That's why *The Inner Peace Revolution* provides a **clear roadmap** to ensure real, sustainable change. Our approach is built on three essential pillars:

- **STRUCTURE:** A guided pathway that eliminates guesswork and helps you navigate your journey with clarity and confidence. Knowing where you are and where you're headed is crucial for lasting transformation.
- **SIMPLICITY:** Change doesn't have to be overwhelming. We break everything down into manageable, intuitive steps that

fit seamlessly into your daily life, ensuring that progress feels natural and achievable.

- **SUPPORT:** You don't have to do this alone. *The Inner Peace Revolution* is a space where you feel seen, heard, and held, whether through community, mentorship, or deepening your connection to your own heart and intuition.

This is what makes *The Inner Peace Revolution* different. It's not about fixing yourself or following someone else's version of success. It's about **reclaiming your own rhythm, your own truth, and your own peace**, and knowing that you are fully supported in the process.

THE RHYTHM OF CHANGE

Life has a natural rhythm, and so do you. When you're aligned with that rhythm, everything flows more effortlessly. You make decisions with confidence, navigate challenges with grace, and feel a sense of peace that's not dependent on external circumstances. But when you're out of sync, when you're rushing, overthinking, or striving for perfection, life feels like an uphill battle.

There are moments in life that force you to pause and reassess where you are and where you're going. Sometimes, these moments come gradually, a slow realisation that something no longer fits. Other times, they arrive as abrupt, undeniable shifts: children leaving home, a career change, the end of a relationship, or a health crisis that demands your attention. These transitions can feel unsettling, like standing at a fork in the road with no clear direction forward. The roles and identities that once defined you may no longer feel aligned, leaving you with a lingering question—Who am I now?

This is where true transformation begins. Not in rushing to fill the space with the next thing but in embracing the pause, the recalibration, and the opportunity to listen deeply to yourself. It's in these seasons of change that the invitation to realign with your authentic rhythm becomes the most profound. When you give yourself permission to lean into the unknown, you create space to rediscover what truly lights you up and to build a life that reflects who you are becoming, not just who you have been.

Our work is about helping women reconnect with their rhythm. It's not about giving you a step by step formula or asking you to fit into a pre-designed mold. It's about guiding you to rediscover the unique cadence of your life and supporting you as you create a sustainable, fulfilling way of being.

We do this through a blend of practical tools and deep inner work. Imagine creating daily habits that nourish your body, mind, and spirit. Picture pausing for just five minutes each day to connect with your breath, reflect on what you're grateful for, or tune into how your body feels. These small, intentional practices may seem simple, but they're incredibly powerful. Over time, they create ripples of change that transform not just how you feel but how you live.

For Patsy, the wake-up call came in a stark, sterile hospital room, with someone else's blood flowing into her arm. Years of ignoring her body's whispers had led to a health crisis so severe that she found herself needing a blood transfusion. She had always told herself she would slow down after she reached the next milestone, after her work was done, after everyone else's needs were met, she was seeking validation outside. But that moment never came. She had placed loyalty to others above loyalty to herself, believing that pushing through exhaustion was a sign of strength. Play, rest, and self-love had been luxuries, things she would get to eventually, when there was time. But life had other plans. Lying there, she realised that the time to care for herself wasn't in the distant future. It was now.

That moment marked a turning point, the beginning of a journey back to her natural rhythm, back to life with energy. She began prioritising her health, making conscious choices to nourish her body and mind, not as a reward, but as an essential part of life. She

119

learned that true loyalty begins with honoring yourself first, filling up your own cup first. She re-evaluated her commitments, recognising that overworking and proving herself had kept her from the deeper fulfillment she longed for. Through guidance from coaches and mentors, she began aligning her life with her values and rediscovering the joy of simply being. She made space for stillness, where she could hear the quiet wisdom of her soul, guiding her toward a life of ease, flow, and peacefulness. It wasn't about achieving more, it was about becoming more of herself.

WHY WHAT YOU'VE TRIED ALREADY... HASN'T ALREADY WORKED

Many of the women we work with come to us after years of trying to "fix" themselves through diets, self-help books, or endless to-do lists. You've followed the rules, done the work, tried everything the experts told you to do. You've journaled, made vision boards, set goals, and powered through. But no matter how hard you push, it still feels like something is missing. That's because traditional approaches focus on surface-level change, fixing the symptoms rather than healing the root. They teach you to do more, not to be more."

But despite their best efforts, they still feel exhausted, disconnected, and stuck in a cycle that never quite leads to the change they desire. The reason these methods often fail is simple: they don't honor the rhythm of your life. They push you to force change instead of flowing with it. They're rigid where you need flexibility, chaotic where you crave structure, and isolating when what you truly need is connection.

Most traditional approaches focus on **external solutions**, fixing the symptoms rather than addressing the deeper patterns that created them in the first place. A new diet might promise confidence, but it doesn't address the emotional weight you carry. A productivity hack might help you get more done, but it doesn't ease the overwhelm in your heart. A self-help book might inspire you, but without integration, the wisdom stays on the pages instead of becoming a lived experience.

The truth is, transformation doesn't happen through sheer willpower. It happens when you **slow down enough to tune into the pulse of your life**, to listen to what your body, mind, and spirit are trying to tell you. It's about creating space for clarity, embracing curiosity, and aligning with the deeper truths that have always been there, waiting for you to notice.

Instead of pushing harder, what if you leaned into trust? Instead of searching for the next quick fix, what if you tuned into your natural rhythm? Instead of constantly trying to fix yourself, what if you accepted that you were never broken to begin with?

The work we do isn't about adding more to your plate or asking you to do more, it's about unlearning the patterns that have kept you disconnected from yourself. It's about **returning to your body, your intuition, your heart space**.

That's why what you've tried before hasn't worked, because real transformation isn't about forcing change. It's about **allowing change**. It's about stepping into flow, embracing who you are, and learning how to work with yourself instead of against yourself.

For Rae, it was heartbreak that cracked her wide open. She had poured herself into a relationship, believing she could fix someone else's brokenness, only to find herself shattered in the process. The emotional and physical toll left her questioning not only her worth but her very identity. In the midst of the wreckage, she discovered something profound: the person she needed to save was herself. It wasn't about fixing; it was about rediscovering and nurturing her own light. Once Rae surrendered and began to trust in herself again, she leaned into the woman she wanted to become, living from a place of intuition and connection to source. She formed relationships with people who truly valued and loved her for who she was, and sought mentors who gave her the confidence to share her journey. Rae's rediscovery of her light not only transformed her life but also inspired her to guide others in shining their own.

THE INNER PEACE REVOLUTION AND THE POWER OF THE SUPERCONSCIOUS

At the heart of *The Inner Peace Revolution* is the understanding that true transformation goes beyond the conscious mind. It's not just about changing habits or adopting new routines; it's about tapping into something deeper, something greater. This is where the concept of the Superconscious becomes a vital part of our work.

To fully grasp the power of the Superconscious, it helps to understand the three levels of consciousness that shape our thoughts, behaviors, and experiences:

- **EGO (CONSCIOUS MIND):** This is the surface level of awareness, the part of us that navigates daily decisions, analyses information, and interacts with the external world. The ego often seeks control, structure, and validation, keeping us in a state of doing rather than being. While necessary for practical life, when the ego dominates, we can become trapped in patterns of overthinking, stress, and self-doubt.

- **UNCONSCIOUS MIND:** The unconscious mind stores our past experiences, beliefs, and conditioned responses. It operates beneath our awareness, running automated patterns that shape how we perceive ourselves and the world. Many of the challenges we experience, fears, doubts, and ingrained habits, stem from unconscious programming that was formed early in life. While the unconscious holds great wisdom, it can also keep us stuck in outdated patterns unless we learn to work with it consciously.

- **SUPERCONSCIOUS (HIGHER MIND):** This is the expansive, intuitive part of you that connects to wisdom, purpose, and possibility. Unlike the ego, which is bound by logic and past experiences, the Superconscious offers a broader perspective, one that aligns with your highest self. It is the part of you that knows your true path and offers guidance when you create space to listen.

WHY WE FOCUS ON THE SUPERCONSCIOUS

In our work, we guide women to access their Superconscious mind to gain clarity, shift perspectives, and create aligned action. Unlike traditional methods that focus solely on mindset or behavior, our approach integrates this higher level of awareness to ensure that transformation happens on a deeper level, one that feels natural, expansive, and aligned with who you truly are.

When you learn to tap into the Superconscious, you move beyond the limitations of the ego and unconscious mind. Instead of reacting based on past fears or over analysing decisions, you begin to trust your intuition and develop a greater sense of inner knowing. This shift allows you to experience more ease, clarity, and alignment in your daily life.

BRINGING IT ALL TOGETHER

When you align with the wisdom of your Superconscious, you move from struggle to flow. You begin to trust your intuition, make empowered choices, and cultivate a life that feels not only peaceful but purposeful. The journey to inner peace isn't just about doing, it's about *being*, and by harnessing the power of your Superconscious, you unlock the ability to live in greater alignment with yourself.

Through *The Inner Peace Revolution*, we help women break free from the mental loops of the ego, shift outdated unconscious patterns, and step into their higher knowing. This isn't about pushing or forcing change, it's about allowing transformation to unfold naturally, in alignment with who you truly are. And when you learn to work with the Superconscious, life stops feeling like a battle and starts feeling more in sync with your true essence.

THE POWER OF PERSPECTIVE

MEET CAROL: SHIFTING PERSPECTIVES TO FIND TRUE ALIGNMENT

"Have you ever felt like you were on the right path, only to wake up one day feeling trapped by the very life you built? That was Carol's reality."

When Carol came to us, she was at a crossroads. After dedicating over 30 years to a high-level corporate career, tirelessly managing large-scale projects, driving strategic initiatives, and navigating the relentless pressure of executive leadership, she felt unfulfilled. The long hours, often stretching late into the night, left little room for anything beyond work. She was highly regarded in her industry, with a solid reputation and the weight of her decisions influencing major business outcomes. Yet, despite her expertise and the respect she commanded, the joy she once felt had faded.

Carol was exhausted, physically and emotionally. Burnout had crept in, and she was no longer looking after herself. She felt trapped within the very system she had once loved, scared to step away from the security and familiarity of her career. The thought of leaving behind her decades of experience, professional credibility, and financial stability was daunting. But deep down, she yearned for something more, *fun, freedom, and flexibility*. She wanted a life where she could still make an impact but without sacrificing herself in the process.

Through our work together, we focused on shifting Carol's perspective, helping her step back from the fear and self-doubt clouding her vision. We introduced techniques to connect her with her superconscious mind, guiding her to access a space of clarity and deeper truth. From this elevated perspective, she began to see her situation not as an ending, but as an invitation to realign with her true desires.

In this newfound space of possibility, Carol uncovered the deeper purpose behind her work: creating meaningful impact without being confined by the rigid structures of corporate bureaucracy. She realised that the skills she had honed, streamlining complex business strategies, fostering collaboration, and navigating high-pressure leadership environments, were not limited to her corporate role. They were valuable assets she could take with her into a new chapter.

With this shift in perspective, Carol made the courageous decision to leave behind the late nights, the constant pressure, and the bureaucratic red tape that once defined her life. Instead, she embraced the freedom to design a career on her own terms. She launched her own consulting business, advising community-based businesses and private sector leaders on developing impactful policies—*but this time, from the comfort of her home.*

Today, Carol enjoys a fulfilling career that gives her the *balance* she once thought was impossible. She has the *flexibility* to prioritise her health, relationships, and hobbies. She's discovered a newfound sense of *fun*, filling her days with activities she had long neglected, morning walks, creative pursuits, and spontaneous getaways that were once unimaginable in her old life.

Carol's journey is proof that when you shift your perspective and connect with your superconscious, the possibilities are limitless. What once felt like an impossible leap became a graceful transition into a life she loves.

We know that a shift in perspective can change everything. Your next chapter is waiting, you just need to see it differently.

The reason why one of the most significant shifts our clients experience is because many come to us feeling trapped by their circumstances, believing their struggles are insurmountable. But what if the stories you've been telling yourself about your life aren't the whole truth? What if there's a new, more empowering way to see your situation?

We often share the example of a tissue box to illustrate this concept. From one angle, it looks like a rectangle; from another, it's a square. Both perspectives are valid, yet neither tells the whole story. When you shift your viewpoint, you open yourself to new possibilities.

THE GIFT OF PLAYFULNESS

Another key element of *The Inner Peace Revolution* is **Playfulness**. Too often, personal growth is framed as serious, heavy work. While there are certainly moments that require deep introspection, we've found that curiosity and lightheartedness are equally important.

When you approach life with a sense of wonder and openness, you create space for new insights to emerge. Another one of our beautiful clients Sara, for years, she held back her playfulness and love for dance, believing it wasn't something she could pursue authentically. She felt disconnected from her true self, trapped by limiting beliefs and societal expectations.

Through our work together, Sara broke through the barriers holding her back. She finally gave herself permission to move her body freely and enrolled in an 80's dance class. What started as a fun experiment soon became a profound reconnection with her inner joy. Encouraged by the freedom she felt, she took it a step further and became a certified dance instructor.

By embracing playfulness, Sara unlocked more flow and expansion in all areas of her life. She released long-held energy blocks, gained confidence, and found a renewed sense of purpose. Playfulness, she discovered, wasn't just about dancing, it was about living life with more ease, creativity, and authenticity.

This playfulness is what sets our work apart from other coaches. We blend structure, simplicity, and support. We don't believe in quick fixes or one-size-fits-all solutions. Instead, we provide a roadmap that's clear enough to guide you but flexible enough to adapt to your unique journey. Our tools are designed to be simple yet profound, helping you integrate meaningful practices into your daily life without adding to your overwhelm. And perhaps most importantly, we create a space where you feel fully seen, heard, and supported.

As you have read… We have walked this path ourselves. We've navigated the burnout, the self-doubt, and the fear of stepping into the unknown. We've learned the hard way that true transformation isn't about fixing what's "wrong" but reconnecting with what's already right. And we've seen firsthand how powerful this work can be, not just in our own lives but in the lives of the women we've been privileged to guide.

YOUR INVITATION TO BEGIN

If you've felt that whisper, that gentle nudge calling you to explore what's next, we want you to know that you are not alone. You are exactly where you are meant to be, standing at the threshold of something new, a life that feels aligned, fulfilling, and deeply connected to who you truly are.

Stepping into transformation doesn't require giant leaps or overwhelming changes. The first step doesn't have to be massive. It can be as simple as taking a breath, writing one word of gratitude, or choosing presence in a moment of chaos. True, lasting shifts begin with the smallest of choices, the decision to pause, to take a breath, to lean into what's possible. *The Inner Peace Revolution* was created to guide you through this journey, offering the structure, simplicity, and support to help you cultivate meaningful change in a way that feels natural and sustainable.

One of the most powerful ways to begin is by tuning into the rhythm of your own life. That's why we invite you to start with our Daily Rhythm Tracker, a free tool designed to help you create small, intentional habits that align with your unique flow. With just a few minutes each day, you will begin to shift your focus, reconnect with your inner wisdom, and lay the foundation for lasting transformation.

This isn't about adding more to your plate, it's about integrating what truly matters. The tracker is your gentle reminder to return to yourself, to move through your days with more presence and purpose. Whether it's a mindful breath, a moment of gratitude, or a pause to feel into your heart space, these small steps ripple outwards, creating profound shifts over time.

The best part? You don't have to do this alone. *The Inner Peace Revolution* is here to walk alongside you, to remind you that you are supported, seen, and capable of creating a life that feels both peaceful and powerful.

Your path to inner peace is already unfolding, one breath, one moment, one rhythm at a time. Trust it, embrace it, and know that the best is yet to come.

Are you ready to begin? Access your Daily Rhythm Tracker here: **https://theinnerpeacerevolution.com/daily-rythm-7-day-tracker-page**

Book a coffee chat with us. We would love to connect: **https://link.coachflowsystems.com/widget/bookings/scc-coffee-call**

www.ingramcontent.com/pod-product-compliance
Lightning Source LLC
Chambersburg PA
CBHW061654120626
46550CB00003B/938